G000129268

An Analysis of

Aristotle's

Nicomachean Ethics

Giovanni Gellera
with
Jon W. Thompson

www.macat.com
info@macat.com

Cover illustration: Etienne Gilfillan

Cataloguing in Publication Data
A catalogue record for this book is available from the British Library.
Library of Congress Cataloguing-in-Publication Data is available upon request.

ISBN 978-1-912302-96-3 (hardback)
ISBN 978-1-912127-95-5 (paperback)
ISBN 978-1-912281-84-8 (e-book)

Notice
The information in this book is designed to orientate readers of the work under analysis,
to elucidate and contextualise its key ideas and themes, and to aid in the development
of critical thinking skills. It is not meant to be used, nor should it be used, as a
substitute for original thinking or in place of original writing or research. References and
notes are provided for informational purposes and their presence does not constitute
endorsement of the information or opinions therein. This book is presented solely for
educational purposes. It is sold on the understanding that the publisher is not engaged
to provide any scholarly advice. The publisher has made every effort to ensure that
this book is accurate and up-to-date, but makes no warranties or representations with
regard to the completeness or reliability of the information it contains. The information
and the opinions provided herein are not guaranteed or warranted to produce particular
results and may not be suitable for students of every ability. The publisher shall not be
liable for any loss, damage or disruption arising from any errors or omissions, or from
the use of this book, including, but not limited to, special, incidental, consequential or
other damages caused, or alleged to have been caused, directly or indirectly, by the
information contained within.

CONTENTS

THE MACAT LIBRARY

The Macat Library is a series of unique academic explorations of seminal works in the humanities and social sciences – books and papers that have had a significant and widely recognised impact on their disciplines. It has been created to serve as much more than just a summary of what lies between the covers of a great book. It illuminates and explores the influences on, ideas of, and impact of that book. Our goal is to offer a learning resource that encourages critical thinking and fosters a better, deeper understanding of important ideas.

Each publication is divided into three Sections: Influences, Ideas, and Impact. Each Section has four Modules. These explore every important facet of the work, and the responses to it.

This Section-Module structure makes a Macat Library book easy to use, but it has another important feature. Because each Macat book is written to the same format, it is possible (and encouraged!) to cross-reference multiple Macat books along the same lines of inquiry or research. This allows the reader to open up interesting interdisciplinary pathways.

To further aid your reading, lists of glossary terms and people mentioned are included at the end of this book (these are indicated by an asterisk [*] throughout) – as well as a list of works cited.

Macat has worked with the University of Cambridge to identify the elements of critical thinking and understand the ways in which six different skills combine to enable effective thinking.
Three allow us to fully understand a problem; three more give us the tools to solve it. Together, these six skills make up the **PACIER** model of critical thinking. They are:

ANALYSIS – understanding how an argument is built
EVALUATION – exploring the strengths and weaknesses of an argument
INTERPRETATION – understanding issues of meaning

CREATIVE THINKING – coming up with new ideas and fresh connections
PROBLEM-SOLVING – producing strong solutions
REASONING – creating strong arguments

To find out more, visit **WWW.MACAT.COM.**

CRITICAL THINKING AND *NICOMACHEAN ETHICS*

Primary critical thinking skill: REASONING
Secondary critical thinking skill: EVALUATION

In *Nicomachean Ethics*, Aristotle shows himself to be a fine example of a thinker whose writing is clearly and coherently reasoned.

Very much concerned with identifying the features of ethical behaviour, Aristotle wanted to know what makes an ethical life. Providing, as he does, epic, rigorously-reasoned arguments, the Greek thinker is generally recognised as a 'difficult' philosopher. But what can be taken for difficulty – the density and persistence of his argumentation – can also be seen as a strong feature of its clarity. He uses hypothetical argumentation to good effect: if a man has one of the virtues, then he must have all of them since, if he has a fully developed virtue, then he has 'practical wisdom;' if he has such wisdom, then he has all the virtues.

Aristotle also deals with counter-arguments in his reasoning. In his argument for the good (or successful) life, he carefully argues against Plato's Idea of the Good on the basis that it's not achievable and, anyway, it is not something that fits with Aristotle's stress on the virtue of achieving success in politics, economics and wisdom. His careful argumentation also pays close attention to the meaning of the terms that he uses, such as 'practical wisdom' and 'political wisdom'. The unique product of a rich deployment of key critical thinking skills, *Nicomachean Ethics* comprises a rich exploration of virtue, reason and the ultimate human good – an exploration, moreover, that forms the basis of the values that lie at the heart of Western civilization to this day.

ABOUT THE AUTHOR OF THE ORIGINAL WORK

Aristotle was born in 384 BCE, in what is present-day Macedonia. At the age of 17 he moved to Athens in Greece to begin an education in philosophy under Plato, one of the founders of European philosophy, at his renowned Academy. On Plato's death in 347 BCE, Aristotle moved back to Macedonia to tutor the young Alexander the Great. But in 335 BCE he returned to Athens and established his own school, the Lyceum. Political unrest forced Aristotle to leave Athens again in 322 BCE, and he died shortly afterwards on the island of Euboea.

ABOUT THE AUTHORS OF THE ANALYSIS

Dr Giovanni Gellera holds a doctorate from the University of Glasgow on the reception of Aristotle in seventeenth-century Scotland. He is curently a postdoctoral researcher in early modern philosophy and science at his alma mater.

Jon W. Thompson teaches in the Department of Philosophy at King's College London, where he is currently a PhD candidate.

ABOUT MACAT

GREAT WORKS FOR CRITICAL THINKING

Macat is focused on making the ideas of the world's great thinkers accessible and comprehensible to everybody, everywhere, in ways that promote the development of enhanced critical thinking skills.

It works with leading academics from the world's top universities to produce new analyses that focus on the ideas and the impact of the most influential works ever written across a wide variety of academic disciplines. Each of the works that sit at the heart of its growing library is an enduring example of great thinking. But by setting them in context – and looking at the influences that shaped their authors, as well as the responses they provoked – Macat encourages readers to look at these classics and game-changers with fresh eyes. Readers learn to think, engage and challenge their ideas, rather than simply accepting them.

'Macat offers an amazing first-of-its-kind tool for interdisciplinary learning and research. Its focus on works that transformed their disciplines and its rigorous approach, drawing on the world's leading experts and educational institutions, opens up a world-class education to anyone.'

Andreas Schleicher
Director for Education and Skills, Organisation for Economic
Co-operation and Development

'Macat is taking on some of the major challenges in university education … They have drawn together a strong team of active academics who are producing teaching materials that are novel in the breadth of their approach.'

Prof Lord Broers,
former Vice-Chancellor of the University of Cambridge

'The Macat vision is exceptionally exciting. It focuses upon new modes of learning which analyse and explain seminal texts which have profoundly influenced world thinking and so social and economic development. It promotes the kind of critical thinking which is essential for any society and economy. This is the learning of the future.'

Rt Hon Charles Clarke, former UK Secretary of State for Education

'The Macat analyses provide immediate access to the critical conversation surrounding the books that have shaped their respective discipline, which will make them an invaluable resource to all of those, students and teachers, working in the field.'

Professor William Tronzo, University of California at San Diego

WAYS IN TO THE TEXT

KEY POINTS

- Aristotle was born in 384 B.C.E. in Stagira, Greece. He is one of the greatest philosophers* in history.

- In his *Nicomachean Ethics*, composed between 335 and 322 B.C.E., Aristotle argues that happiness is the greatest good, and that real happiness is achieved by ethically* good action ("ethics" is the branch of philosophy concerned with the question "How should one live?").

- Aristotle's *Nicomachean Ethics* stresses that ethically good action springs from the virtues* (a term referring to dispositions of character and action) of moral character and intellect.

Who Was Aristotle?

Aristotle, the author of *Nicomachean Ethics* (composed between 335 and 322 B.C.E.), was a philosopher of ancient Greece. One of the most famous thinkers of all time, he was born in Stagira, a town in Macedonia, a kingdom north of classical Greece. Aristotle's father was a physician named Nicomachus; his mother was named Phaestis. When Aristotle turned 18, he moved to Athens, the center of learning in the Greek world, where he studied with the great philosopher Plato* at the Academy*—Plato's famed center of philosophical learning. Aristotle remained at the Academy until 348 B.C.E., and in 343 B.C.E. became the personal tutor to the young Alexander the

Great.* Son of King Philip II of Macedonia, Alexander became a military leader and ruler of an enormous empire incorporating Greece.

On his return to Athens, Aristotle established his own school for the education of notable youth, the Lyceum,* in 335 B.C.E.; on account of the *peripatos*, a circular place for walking, nearby, Aristotle's followers are often called Peripatetics.* During his time as master of the Lyceum school, Aristotle lectured his students on a wide range of subjects, including politics, physics, poetry, and logic* (the subfield of philosophy concerned with methodical, rational reasoning). After a long and productive career, he died at the age of 62 on the Greek island of Euboea, in 322 B.C.E.

Aristotle devoted his life to learning, investigating nature, and passing on this knowledge to students. His status as one of the most important thinkers of all time is largely due to the survival of some of his most influential and systematic philosophical works. He also created two new fields: logic and biology* (the study of living things). Much of Aristotle's work focused on ethics, or the study of right and wrong, and *Nicomachean Ethics*, named after his father, is a timeless philosophical classic. As one commentator has noted, "Aristotle holds a position of unparalleled importance in the history of philosophy—and he is a thunderingly good philosopher to boot."[1] Many of the moral concepts and principles of what we now think of as the West* (primarily Europe, North America, and Australia–New Zealand) can be traced back to *Nicomachean Ethics*, and to the Aristotelian concepts of happiness, virtue, and practical wisdom.

What Does *Nicomachean Ethics* Say?

Although now considered one of history's first great ethical treatises* (systematic written analyses), *Nicomachean Ethics* was not published by Aristotle himself. Rather, one of Aristotle's students is likely to have organized it from a set of lecture notes Aristotle wrote for the Lyceum between 335 and 322 B.C.E. In any case, the work has profoundly influenced every era of moral philosophy* since Aristotle's day ("moral philosophy" is the branch of philosophy concerned with the theory and practice of morality—that is, with the question "How ought we to live?").

Most current editions of *Nicomachean Ethics* include 10 books and chapter divisions within the books. The division into books goes back to the oldest known versions of *Nicomachean Ethics*, but the chapters are more modern subdivisions. When the work is cited as *Nicomachean Ethics*, the citation is split into two parts, commonly taking the form "X.7.1177a13–18"; in this example, the first part ("X.7") refers to Book 10 and chapter 7 in the translation by the scholar Roger Crisp;[2] often this will be the only citation given. When the second part is used ("1177a13–18"), it corresponds to the text citation system devised by the German philosopher August Immanuel Bekker* in 1831. Using the second part, a student should be able to find the passage in virtually any translation of Aristotle's works.

Nicomachean Ethics investigates the question of what a good human life is. In answering this question, Aristotle argues that a good life is one conducted according to the function or purpose (Greek: *ergon*)* of human nature.

In Aristotle's sense, a "function" is a thing's unique and defining purpose. The function of a knife, for example, is to cut, and the function of a hammer is to hit things. Aristotle asks himself the following question: "What is the function of human beings?"—in other words, what are human beings meant to do?

Aristotle believes that mankind's highest function is *eudaimonia*—happiness, or flourishing. But what does this happiness consist of?

For Aristotle, our function as human beings will be determined by what separates us from other things in the world: reason* (the human faculty of abstract reflection). As human beings, we can exercise reason regarding both theoretical and practical matters. So, our function—

and therefore the key to real *eudaimonia*—is to be realized through the proper exercise of theoretical and practical reason.

For Aristotle, the proper exercise of theoretical and practical reason was a question of recognizing the middle way between extremes of action and character; practical reason demands that people be neither cowardly nor rash in the face of danger. The mean* (that is, the desired middle) between these two extremes is the character trait of courage. These "middle way" character traits are called "virtues," and Aristotle outlines many, including justice, courage, temperance* (that is, restraint, usually with regard to pleasurable activities), and practical wisdom.

Aristotle does not omit a discussion of theoretical reason. Toward the end of *Nicomachean Ethics*, he returns to contemplation* (for him, reflection on eternal truths), a practice he considers the highest realization of *eudaimonia*. He writes in Book X.7–8: "If happiness is activity in accordance with virtue, it is reasonable to expect that it is in accordance with the highest virtue ... [T]his activity is that of contemplation."[3]

It is best to consider the central social or political aspect of *Nicomachean Ethics* as continuous with Aristotle's other major work on practical matters, *Politics*. In that work, Aristotle produces the famous definition of man as a "political animal" (*Politics*, 1253a1–4):[4] our lives are social by nature, and we need the companionship of other humans to achieve happiness. Further, the goal of a group of individuals runs parallel to the goal of the individual. So the noble goal of politicians ought to be producing the material conditions for the well-being and happiness of the citizens, just as the goal of the individual is to attain the virtues necessary for his own happiness.

Why Does *Nicomachean Ethics* Matter?

The impact of *Nicomachean Ethics* and of Aristotle's arguments is perhaps unparalleled in the history of philosophy. The philosophy professor Terence Irwin* of Oxford University has said that "we can follow one significant thread through the history of moral philosophy by considering how far Aristotle is right, and what his successors think about his claims."[5] Aristotle was called simply "the Philosopher" by medieval* thinkers. Even today, his ideas stand the test of time. Virtue ethics*—a branch of ethics that principally focuses on moral character—is now a leading current in contemporary moral philosophy.[6] The philosopher Rosalind Hursthouse* of New Zealand has written, "Virtue ethics is both an old and a new approach to ethics, old in so far as it dates back to the writings of Plato and, more particularly, Aristotle, new in that, as a revival of this ancient approach, it is a fairly recent addition to contemporary moral theory."[7]

But *Nicomachean Ethics* is not important only for those engaged in academic philosophy. For Aristotle, philosophy begins "because of wonder."[8] There is perhaps no more wondrous set of questions for human beings than that which *Nicomachean Ethics* addresses: What is the nature of happiness or flourishing? How do human beings achieve happiness? And why do human beings fail to achieve happiness? These universal and deeply humane questions guarantee the text's continuing importance.

Finally, when considered together with Aristotle's *Politics*, *Nicomachean Ethics* is still relevant to enduring questions in political and social science. While Aristotle wrote for a culture very different from contemporary global societies, his work can still speak meaningfully to us today; his ethical thought provides a contrast to our modern social and political assumptions. Aristotle is therefore a powerful conversation partner, offering a different perspective on even the most pressing political and economic problems of the contemporary world.[9]

NOTES

1   J. Barnes, *The Cambridge Companion to Aristotle* (Cambridge: Cambridge University Press, 1995), xv.

2   Aristotle, *Nicomachean Ethics*, rev. ed., trans. Roger Crisp (Cambridge: *Cambridge University Press,* 2014).

3   Aristotle, *Nicomachean Ethics*, X.7.1177a.13–18.

4   Aristotle, Politics, trans. T. Irwin, in *Readings in Ancient Greek Philosophy*, eds. S. Cohen, P. Curd and C. D. C. Reeve (Indianapolis: Hackett, 2005), 1253a1–4.

5   T. Irwin, *The Development of Ethics*, vol. 1 (Oxford: Oxford University Press, 2007), 4.

6   Rosalind Hursthouse, "Virtue Ethics," section 2, in *Stanford Encyclopedia of Philosophy*, ed. Edward N. Zalta (Fall 2013 edn.), accessed February 27, 2016, http://plato.stanford.edu/archives/fall2013/entries/ethics-virtue/.

7   Rosalind Hursthouse, *On Virtue Ethics* (Oxford: Oxford University Press, 2001), 9.

8   Aristotle, *Metaphysics*, trans. S. M. Cohen, in *Readings in Ancient Greek Philosophy*, 982b10–15.

9   For a discussion of Aristotle and how his ethics can be revolutionary even today, see Paul Blackledge and Kelvin Knight (eds.), *Virtue and Politics: Alasdair MacIntyre's Revolutionary Aristotelianism* (Notre Dame, IN: University of Notre Dame Press, 2011).

SECTION 1
INFLUENCES

MODULE 1
THE AUTHOR AND THE
HISTORICAL CONTEXT

KEY POINTS

- Dealing with human happiness, Aristotle's *Nicomachean Ethics* is one of the foundational works in moral philosophy.*

- After studying for 20 years with the enormously influential thinker Plato,* Aristotle wrote groundbreaking works of his own.

- A key figure in the intellectual world of ancient Greece, Aristotle taught the military leader Alexander the Great,* who later became ruler of a vast empire.

Why Read this Text?

Aristotle, the author of *Nicomachean Ethics* (composed between 335 and 322 B.C.E.), once asserted that philosophy begins "because of wonder"[1]—the wonder, that is, that we feel in response to the puzzles presented to us in the physical world, in the social world, and in the world of individual human action.

In the text, Aristotle explores some of the most immediate and intimate sources of wonder for human beings—the question of the essential nature and purpose of human beings and the question of how we ought to live. One significant reason to read Aristotle on ethics* is that the text has long been considered foundational for the tradition of ethical reflection in Western thought.

During the Middle Ages* (the fifth to fifteenth centuries C.E.), philosophers usually referred to Aristotle simply as "the Philosopher." *Nicomachean Ethics* is one of the most influential texts in ethics, and a

> ❝ We had perhaps better consider the universal good and discuss thoroughly what is meant by it. ❞
>
> Aristotle, *Nicomachean Ethics*

major new commentary appears approximately every 10 years. This makes it one of the most studied and influential works in the history of Western philosophy. *Nicomachean Ethics* is the first surviving work that systematically investigates the central ethical concerns of human life: What is happiness (*eudaimonia*)* and how can it be achieved?[2] The work established moral philosophy as an independent discipline, and it decisively influenced the field's terminology, main arguments, and structure.

If it is clear that basic needs must be met in order to live, what is it that makes a life *good*? While everyone in Aristotle's day agreed that happiness makes for a good life, there was disagreement about what happiness is. While many considered happiness a matter of pleasure, honor, or wealth, Aristotle followed his teacher, the influential philosopher Plato, in arguing that this was a mistaken idea. Those things are sought as a means to some other end—but the ultimate goal of all human action is the good that people are really aiming at in all of their activities.

Nicomachean Ethics has maintained its relevance in every historical period and has influenced philosophical and political thought up to the present day.

Author's Life

Aristotle was born in 384 B.C.E. in the town of Stagira in what was then known as Macedonia, now a region of northern Greece. His father, Nicomachus, was a physician at the Macedonian court. Nicomachus gave his son the best education available and, being a physician, may have influenced the empirical, scientific emphasis in

Aristotle's philosophical work ("empiricism" is an approach to scientific inquiry founded on information verifiable by observation).

At the age of 17, Aristotle went to Athens to study with Plato at his school, the Academy.*³ He left Athens after Plato's death in 347 B.C.E., and between 347 and 343 B.C.E. he engaged in biological* studies in Asia Minor (modern-day Turkey) and the Aegean islands east of Greece. While living on the Island of Lesbos, Aristotle married a woman named Pythias; the two had a daughter by the same name. He then moved to the Macedonian court, serving for a short time as tutor to Alexander the Great. On his return to Athens in 335 B.C.E., Aristotle founded his own philosophical school, the Lyceum.* Members of this school are known as "Peripatetics," a name derived from the Greek *peripatos* ("ambulatory"),* referring to the covered walking area nearby. Aristotle produced most of his works at the Lyceum and taught there until Alexander's death in 323 B.C.E. Because of his well-known association with the Macedonians, and fearing the anti-Macedonian movement, Aristotle then left Athens, this time for good. He spent the last year of his life on the large Greek island of Euboea, where he died in 322 B.C.E.⁴

Author's Background

Aristotle lived in the ancient Greek city-state (Greek: *polis*)* of Athens for the most important part of his philosophical career. Athens was the most powerful of the hundreds of Greek city-states dotted around the Aegean Sea, and it had survived both the Persian Wars* of the early fifth century B.C.E. and the Peloponnesian War* of the late fifth century B.C.E.—conflicts that deeply shaped the region. Athens is known as the birthplace of democracy*—a system in which rule is in the hands of the people, rather than in the hands of any monarch or elite—but, in practice, only relatively wealthy male citizens were allowed to take part in the political process.

Aristotle lived in Athens during a period of relative political stability and immense cultural advances. Athens' political stability was arguably due to the success of the democratic system in the 80 years following the Peloponnesian War against the rival city-state of Sparta.* This period of general tolerance for both democrats and citizens favoring rule by the elite, provided very important stability for the development of philosophical schools. This was in spite of the fact that in 399 B.C.E. an Athenian jury put to death the influential philosopher Socrates,* who had been the teacher of Aristotle's own teacher Plato, for his "corrupting" philosophical teachings. This famous incident was an important exception to the general rule of tolerance in Athens in the fourth century B.C.E.

Due in part to this political stability, Athens had reached perhaps the highest point in its cultural development, with its most famous artists, sculptors, dramatists, and philosophers working in the fifth and fourth centuries B.C.E. It was within this context that both Plato's Academy and Aristotle's Lyceum flourished. The former was vital for Aristotle's philosophical education, and the latter was necessary for developing and passing on his own philosophical teaching. It was only when Alexander the Great died in 323 B.C.E. that the situation in Athens became a problem for Aristotle; Athenians were wary of their Macedonian neighbors to the north, and the death of Alexander meant that the stability of his empire was no longer a certainty. Tradition holds that Aristotle fled Athens in order that it might not "sin twice" against philosophy by taking his life, having already taken the life of Socrates.

Aristotle's contributions to Athens' philosophical legacy are impressive, as is his advancement of human knowledge more generally. He structured the discipline of philosophy as we know it today,[5] and he established at least two fundamental branches of science: logic* and biology.[6]

NOTES

1   Aristotle, *Metaphysics*, trans. S. M. Cohen, in *Readings in Ancient Greek Philosophy*, eds. S. Cohen, P. Curd and C. D. C. Reeve (Indianapolis, IN: Hackett, 2005), 982b10–15.

2   Richard Kraut, "Two Conceptions of Happiness," *The Philosophical Review 88 (*1979): 167–97.

3   Christopher Shields, "Aristotle," in *Stanford Encyclopedia of Philosophy,* ed. Edward N. Zalta (Fall 2015 edn.), accessed January 19, 2016, http://plato.stanford.edu/archives/fall2015/entries/aristotle/.

4   For a short version of the biography, see J. Barnes, *The Cambridge Companion to Aristotle* (Cambridge: Cambridge University Press, 1995), 1–15.

5   Especially important are his works *Physics*, *On the Soul*, and *Metaphysics*, all found in translation in Jonathan Barnes, *Aristotle Complete Works* (Princeton, NJ: Princeton University Press, 1991).

6   Georgios Anagnostopoulos, "Aristotle's Works and the Development of His Thought," in *A Companion to Aristotle*, ed. Georgios Anagnostopoulos (Oxford: Wiley-Blackwell, 2009).

MODULE 2
ACADEMIC CONTEXT

KEY POINTS

- Aristotle's *Nicomachean Ethics* is the most important and influential work in the field of moral philosophy.*

- The question of what makes a happy life is a central concern to politicians, intellectuals, and ordinary people.

- Aristotle's method is to take popular and traditional accounts of the good life seriously, and to assess them philosophically

The Work In Its Context

Aristotle's *Nicomachean Ethics* appeared at a crucial time in the history of philosophy,* and contributes much to what we call philosophy today. While Greek culture was advanced in many fields—notably literature (poetry, epic, theatre), history, science (geometry, mathematics), music, and architecture—the discipline of philosophy was not yet fully formed. The most important forms of philosophical discussions were the oral (spoken) tradition, famously represented by the philosopher Socrates* (the influential teacher of Aristotle's teacher Plato),* and philosophical poetry, represented by the thinker Heraclitus.* Plato was the first to write extensively on philosophy in the form of dialogues (roughly, narratives of ideas conducted through characters speaking to each other), usually with Socrates as the leading character. Philosophy gradually became a discipline independent from literature and poetry; it addressed many of the same problems (life, death, happiness, the origin and nature of the world, ethics,* the immortality of the soul), but approached them more rigorously and methodically.

❝ It is now so widely taken for granted that 'ethics' (or 'moral philosophy' as it is sometimes called) is the name of a distinct branch of philosophy that we must constantly force ourselves to remember that this way of carving up the subject had to be invented, and that Aristotle was one of its inventors. ❞

Richard Kraut, Introduction to *The Blackwell Guide to Aristotle's Nicomachean Ethics*

There were three main philosophical schools in Greek philosophy before Aristotle: the Pre-Socratics* (given that name because they pre-dated Socrates); the Sophists* (travelling professional teachers who engaged in public debates on justice, duty, happiness, and civic virtue); and the philosophical tradition of Socrates and Plato—centered at Plato's Academy.* The Pre-Socratics famously investigated nature in their search for the fundamental principles of all things.[1] Some of the more notable Pre-Socratics included the philosophers Heraclitus, Parmenides,* and Empedocles.* Socrates was the first to define philosophy as focused on problems. He did this largely by challenging the Sophists, who were more confident in their assertions about justice and virtue than was justified; while he explored many of the same civic themes as the Sophists, he did so with a critical and humble attitude.

The historian of philosophy Anthony Preus* argues that there was a key turn from Socrates onwards: "Aristotle, inventor of the word 'ethics,' says that 'in time of Socrates, people turned from inquiry into nature, and philosophers turned to political studies and the useful virtues*.'"[2] In other words, the shift from the Pre-Socratics, through the Sophists, to the intellectual approach of Socrates, Plato, and Aristotle was a shift from speculation about the original principles of nature to discussions about the ethical life.

Overview of the Field

Plato's *Republic* was the most important work of moral philosophy before Aristotle. As in most of Plato's dialogues, he has Socrates making the most interesting arguments, and it is often difficult to tell which ideas originate from Socrates and which are the invention of his student, Plato. In *Republic*, Plato explores the virtues in the individual person by first describing the virtues in the ideal society. He divides this imaginary society into the ruler class, the soldier class, and the citizen class. As the roles of classes of people in the well-ordered city correspond to specific virtues, the rulers of the city must be endowed with wisdom (*sophia*);* the protectors of the city, or soldiers, must have courage (*andreia*);* and the members of every class are to possess temperance or moderation (*sophrosune*)* and justice (*dikaiosune*).* The individual, in Plato's thought, is a miniature version of the city-state in whom the virtues of justice, courage, wisdom, and moderation should also be present. Plato anticipates Aristotle's view that there are four essential virtues, and Plato, like Aristotle, emphasizes the vital role of wisdom in ordering the city-state and one's own soul. Because wisdom directs both the city as a whole and the individual person, wisdom gives a unity to both the ideal society and the virtues.

Academic Influences

Although Aristotle developed his own philosophical approach, including terminology, method, and division of disciplines, the influence of Plato and his school on Aristotle's work can hardly be overstated. Plato had founded the Academy, the first school for theoretical research in the Western world,* and some of the most talented researchers of the period were associated with it. Following Socrates' example, Plato often analyzed and criticized the most common views of his day—views put forward in his dialogues as the opinions of the Sophists. Aristotle studied and taught at the Academy until Plato's death, for a period of some 20 years, and consequently, he should be viewed as sharing the approach of Socrates and Plato, especially in *Nicomachean Ethics* and *Politics*. The historian of philosophy Terence Irwin* confirms this fact: "Aristotle places himself in the Socratic tradition by endorsing the critical examination of common moral beliefs in order to identify the puzzles and difficulties they raise. In Plato's early dialogues Socrates raises these puzzles through systematic cross-examination of ordinary beliefs."[3]

This is, of course, compatible with the fact that Aristotle would develop distinctive and divergent views later in his career. After such development, Aristotle critically discusses theories of other members or associates of the Academy in *Nicomachean Ethics*, notably those of Plato and the astronomer and mathematician Eudoxus* and the philosopher Speusippus,* Plato's nephew. Thus, in arriving at his own view, which tends to differ considerably from those of his intellectual mentors and peers, Aristotle often engages fruitfully with his ex-colleagues from the Academy. He also cites examples or quotations from the Pre-Socratics, Plato, Socrates, and the Sophists, as well as from poets and playwrights of the day.

NOTES

1   Alexander Mourelatos (ed.), *The Pre-Socratics: A Collection of Critical Essays* (Princeton, NJ: Princeton University Press, 1993).

2   Anthony Preus, *Historical Dictionary of Ancient Greek Philosophy* (Lanham, MD: Scarecrow Press, 2007), 108.

3   T. Irwin, *The Development of Ethics*, vol. 1 (Oxford: Oxford University Press, 2007), 2.

MODULE 3
THE PROBLEM

KEY POINTS

- Ancient moral philosophers* sought to answer the question "What is happiness?"

- In Aristotle's time it was considered that ordinary people often identified happiness with money or pleasure; politicians identified it with honor; and many philosophers* argued that happiness was a state of the soul.

- Aristotle disagrees with the argument that happiness is a state of the soul; for him, it is activity in accordance with moral and intellectual virtues.*

Core Question

Aristotle begins *Nicomachean Ethics* by asserting, "Every skill and every inquiry, and similarly every action and rational choice, is thought to aim at some good; and so the good has been aptly described as that at which everything aims."[1] Aristotle thus sets up the work's key question with directness and clarity: What is the highest or best good for human beings?

Aristotle assumes that human beings must be aiming at *something* in their actions, and the thing at which all their actions ultimately aim must be consistent with their nature. Two things that guide Aristotle's answer to the question of happiness are reputable opinions (*endoxa*)* and what one can perceive (*phainomena*).* As a general approach in his philosophy, he seeks agreement between reputable previous opinions and daily personal experience.[2]

Aristotle acknowledges in *Nicomachean Ethics* I.4–5 that there is general agreement that the highest good at which humans aim is

> ❝ Most people, I should think, agree about what [the ultimate good] is called, since both the masses and sophisticated people call it happiness, understanding being happy as equivalent with living well and acting well. They disagree about substantive conceptions of happiness. ❞
>
> Aristotle, *Nicomachean Ethics*

eudaimonia:* happiness or flourishing. Here it must be noted that in the ancient world, people conceived of happiness as an objective state of being rather than merely a subjective experience. In this, all ancient theories differ from our modern use of "happiness"—that is, it is a state of being independent of our perception, not something that we define for ourselves by feeling it. Although Aristotle agrees with Plato and the ordinary person that happiness is the ultimate good and must be objective, he also sees that there is wide disagreement about what this happiness consists of. As he acknowledges, "They disagree about substantive conceptions of happiness, the masses giving an account which differs from that of the philosophers."[3]

Aristotle inherits practical disagreement about what is the ultimate good, and he develops a genuinely new idea about the nature of this highest good. He argues that happiness is *an activity,* not a state of being. It is "activity of the soul in accordance with virtue" in a complete life.[4]

The Participants

In his dialogues *Republic* and *Philebus,* Plato suggests that the soul's possession of the virtues is sufficient for happiness (*eudaimonia*). Plato primarily considers the human good as a state of being rather than an activity. For Plato, virtues are character traits possessed within the soul of the individual that can never be taken away by external circumstances. The virtuous person is virtuous, whether or not she or he has an opportunity to express those virtues. Furthermore, Socrates and Plato likened virtue or moral excellence to a craft. It does not matter whether the craftsman enjoys his work or not: as long as the product is good, he has worked well.

Plato argues in *Republic* that strict education for children is necessary if they are to arrive at the virtuous character that creates happiness: since the pull of pleasure and the fear of pain are undeniable for children and young people, they need external authorities such as teachers and parents guiding their behavior and teaching them about the virtues.[5] Finally, the common person's opinion was that happiness consisted of some external good—such as wealth or fame or pleasure—rather than virtue itself.

The Contemporary Debate

In *Nicomachean Ethics* Aristotle begins by considering "reputable" ("*endoxa*") opinions.[6] He advances his own theory only after a detailed and careful analysis of the theories of others, who include philosophers, sages, and poets. Although it is clear that Plato and his teacher Socrates influenced Aristotle the most, the key themes seem to be developed with Plato's view in mind. But Aristotle also paid attention to the ordinary person's opinions about happiness.

Regarding the nature of happiness (*eudaimonia*), Aristotle agrees with Plato that the best life centers on the virtues. But there are important differences between their accounts. Aristotle argues, contrary to Plato, that virtue is necessary, but not sufficient, for *eudaimonia*; it is absurd to argue that the person who is internally virtuous but desperately poor is really happy. Instead, Aristotle draws on the popular insight that there is something important for happiness in wealth and honor, arguing that virtuous *action* and contemplation represent the fullest life of happiness, and admitting that some level of money and health is necessary to achieve this.

Aristotle also develops Plato's understanding of the relationship between virtue and pleasure. In *Nicomachean Ethics*, Aristotle follows Plato in acknowledging that pleasure cannot be the ultimate good, stating that "pleasure is not the good, because the good cannot become more worthy of choice by anything's being added to it."[7] According to both Plato and Aristotle, the life of pure pleasure can be improved by also being characterized by reason—in which case pleasure cannot be *the ultimate good*, since the ultimate good must be incapable of being improved on. Aristotle, however, argues that the full development of virtue will mean that the virtuous person takes pleasure in his virtuous activity, so that doing what is right grudgingly indicates that one is not completely virtuous[8]—a slight adjustment of Plato's position.

There is a final important difference between Plato and Aristotle in regard to ethics.* For Plato, every human action was aimed at the "Form of the Good." This was, for Plato, an abstract concept that united all the things we call "good": a good man, a good intellect, good archery, for example. Though acknowledging that this account has some appeal, Aristotle ultimately disagrees with it, stating that there is no form that all good things (listing the examples of "honor, practical wisdom and pleasure") can meaningfully be said to share.[9] Ethics, therefore, does not require theoretical knowledge of the abstract Form of the Good but only practical wisdom.

NOTES

1   Aristotle, *Nicomachean Ethics*, trans. Roger Crisp (Cambridge: Cambridge University Press, 2014), I.1.1094a,1–3.

2   Aristotle, *Nicomachean Ethics*, VII.I.1145b2–7; cf. Christopher Shields, "Aristotle," *Stanford Encyclopedia of Philosophy*, ed. Edward N. Zalta (Fall 2015 edn.), accessed January 19, 2016, http://plato.stanford.edu/archives/fall2015/entries/aristotle/.

3   Aristotle, *Nicomachean Ethics*, I.4.1095a,16-22.

4   Aristotle, *Nicomachean Ethics*, I.7.1098a16–18.

5   Aristotle, *Nicomachean Ethics*, X.9.1179b16–18 and II.3.1104b12–13.

6   Aristotle, *Nicomachean Ethics*, I.4-5 for some remarks on the method and the assessment of *endoxa*.

7   Aristotle, *Nicomachean Ethics*, 1172b28 ff; Plato, *Philebus*, 60c-61a.

8   Aristotle, *Nicomachean Ethics*, II.3.1104b3–11.

9   Aristotle, *Nicomachean Ethics*, I.6.1096b24; the full argument is found in I.6.1096b10–35.

MODULE 4
THE AUTHOR'S CONTRIBUTION

KEY POINTS

- In *Nicomachean Ethics*, Aristotle considers whether happiness is the highest good of human life, and if so, what is necessary to achieve happiness.

- Aristotle argues that virtue* is necessary, but not sufficient, for happiness; for him, happiness requires virtuous activity, not simply a virtuous state of the soul.

- He draws this insight from combining the ethical theories of the philosopher* Plato* with the beliefs of the common people.

Author's Aims

Aristotle's aim in *Nicomachean Ethics* was to find the highest good of human life,[1] so as to provide both individuals and politicians with a goal and a model of action.[2] It was conventional wisdom that happiness or well-being (*eudaimonia*)* was the thing that every human being aimed at. For Aristotle and other Classical philosophers, *eudaimonia* describes a set of objective facts about the person, rather than merely a passing feeling or opinion of one's life. Some held that happiness is found in wealth, while others located it in honor, and still others in power. However, Aristotle's philosophical predecessors, Plato and Socrates,* had argued that happiness resides in the possession of virtue. Aristotle's inventive approach is to seek to blend these seemingly incompatible conceptions of happiness.

He does so by emphasizing that human good is found in the *exercise* of the virtues, stating that the ultimate good is "activity of the soul in accordance with virtue, and if there are several virtues, in accordance with the best and most complete."[3] But while the

> 66 If ... we take the characteristic activity of a human being to be a certain kind of life; and if we take this kind of life to be activity of the soul and actions in accordance with reason ... and a characteristic activity to be accomplished well when it is accomplished in accordance with the appropriate virtue; then if this is so, the human good turns out to be activity of the soul in accordance with virtue, and if there are several virtues, in accordance with the best and most complete. 99
>
> Aristotle, *Nicomachean Ethics*

possession of a virtue or the virtues is necessary for happiness, it is not sufficient. One must also possess the external things (such as friendship, financial resources, and so on) that are necessary to act in a virtuous manner. Without these, one's virtuous character does not have the chance to be expressed. For instance, if a person aims at practicing the virtue of generosity but possesses only enough money to buy personal food and shelter, then they will not be able to act with that virtue. The stress on virtuous *activity* reveals Aristotle's originality. Therefore, it is wrong to characterize Aristotle's approach as focused on good character as opposed to right action: Aristotle argues that both are necessary for happiness.

The above sheds some light on Aristotle's "virtue ethics"* (his approach to an ethical theory that maintains that the morality of an action should be judged by the character or virtue of the person, rather than by the outcome of the action).

Approach

Aristotle's approach to ethics* in *Nicomachean Ethics* is groundbreaking in two ways: in his practical focus, and in his belief that ethical reflection requires ethical education.

Aristotle also develops a more practical approach to ethics than that of his teacher Plato. Aristotle saw that, since human action and society are full of unforeseen events and luck, we cannot approach ethics as an abstract subject. Ethics is practical. So, whereas Plato had suggested a single term covering theoretical and practical wisdom (Greek: *sophia*),* Aristotle divides the intellect into theoretical wisdom (*sophia*), practical wisdom (*phronesis*),* and productive wisdom (skill in producing things). So one need not be a philosopher or theoretically minded to possess virtues such as justice, courage, or temperance.*[4]

Furthermore, Aristotle's approach to ethics differs both from that of his predecessor Plato and from most modern approaches to the subject in not beginning with a theoretical defense of ethical concepts. We might assume, for instance, that Aristotle would begin with an account not only of why happiness consists of virtuous activity, but also of why the traditional characteristics (justice, temperance, courage) count as virtues at all. Such an account would demonstrate to everyone why they should be just and temperate. Indeed, in *Republic*, Plato uses reason to seek a description of virtues such as justice.[5]

Seeking to understand why Aristotle does not address this question, we should consider that, for Aristotle, knowledge of what is and what is not a virtue is decided in the early stages of one's development. As he states several times, a person can be ruined for life with regard to virtue if he or she is not taught early to exercise discipline in pursuing his or her desires; "anyone," he states, "who is going to be a competent student in the spheres of what is noble and what is just … must be brought up well in his habits."[6] While we can later reflect on and refine our understanding of the virtues, we must learn early on to see their essential nature and that they are ultimately worth pursuing.

Contribution in Context

The main argument of *Nicomachean Ethics* concerns the ultimate human good. This good is agreed to consist of happiness, and Aristotle will conclude that happiness is virtuous, rational activity.[7] But he acknowledges the role of the debate in contemporary Athenian philosophy about the nature of happiness; his response to this debate can be viewed as both a critique and a combining of the prevailing opinions about happiness. Aristotle critiques the views of the common people, who think happiness consists of the possession of "pleasure, wealth, or honor."[8] He argues that such things are only ever pursued for the sake of something else. Money, for instance, is pursued for what it can buy a person, so it cannot be the thing at which all human actions are aimed.

Second, Aristotle disagrees with his philosophical predecessors, Plato and Socrates, about whether virtuous character is sufficient for happiness. While the possession of virtue is necessary, it simply cannot be that someone who is virtuous but is "terribly ugly, of low birth, or solitary and childless" has achieved *eudaimonia* (happiness or well-being).[9] Aristotle arguably blends the best aspects of the conventional opinions about happiness. Plato and Socrates were correct that a human being needs virtuous character to be happy, and the common person's opinions were correct in that money and honor are part of what makes happiness possible. For Aristotle, the happy person is the person who both *possesses* moral and intellectual virtues and has the external goods necessary to *act* in a virtuous way. Finally, Aristotle agrees with Plato that the life of philosophical contemplation is the highest good that human beings can attain.

NOTES

1 Aristotle, *Nicomachean Ethics*, trans. Roger Crisp (Cambridge: Cambridge University Press, 2014), I.2.1094a21–22; and I.4.1095a15–17.

2 Aristotle, *Nicomachean Ethics*, I.2.1094b11.

3 Aristotle, *Nicomachean Ethics*,.7, 1098a,15–16.

4 Aristotle, *Nicomachean Ethics*, VI.3–5.1139b14-1140b30.

5 See, for instance, Plato, *The Republic*, trans. G. M. A. Grube, in *Readings in Ancient Greek Philosophy*, eds. S. Cohen, P. Curd and C. D. C. Reeve (Indianapolis: Hackett, 2005), 336b and following.

6 Aristotle, *Nicomachean Ethics*, I.4.1095b3–5.

7 Aristotle, *Nicomachean Ethics*, I.7, especially 1098a16–17.

8 Aristotle, *Nicomachean Ethics*, I.4, 1095a23–24.

9 Aristotle, *Nicomachean Ethics*, I.8, 1099a31–1099b1–5.

SECTION 2
IDEAS

MODULE 5
MAIN IDEAS

KEY POINTS

- The key themes of *Nicomachean Ethics* are happiness, excellence/virtue,* and action; they require a detailed analysis of good action and character, responsibility, justice, friendship, and pleasure.

- Happiness consists of virtuous activity; complete virtue requires both the virtues of character (courage, for example) and the virtues of intellect, especially practical wisdom.

- Aristotle argues that practical wisdom (Greek: *phronesis*)* helps us determine a mean* (or middle) between extreme character traits, and that each virtue represents such a mean.

Key Themes

The overarching goal of Aristotle's *Nicomachean Ethics* is to give an account of the ultimate human good. Aristotle will argue that virtuous activity is the highest good, and he employs five main concepts to make his argument. These are:

- Happiness (*eudaimonia*) *
- The function (*ergon*)* of human beings
- The excellences or virtues (*aretê*)*
- Practical wisdom (*phronesis*)
- The doctrine* (teaching) of the mean—the desirable middle ground.

In Book I.7, we learn that the most important human good is happiness (*eudaimonia*). This is an *endoxa*—one of the starting points from which a coherent moral philosophy* must be built.

> ❝ Aristotle's *Nicomachean Ethics* is about what is good for human beings. It asks and proposes an answer to the question 'What is the chief or primary good for man?' and looks at the implications of its answer. ❞
>
> Sarah Broadie, "Philosophical Introduction" to Aristotle's *Nicomachean Ethics*

But what does Aristotle understand by "happiness"? It is not merely a subjective emotional state, something we have to define for ourselves as we feel it, as we think of happiness today; rather, it is an objective state—closer to the concept of well-being or human flourishing. Furthermore, happiness or flourishing is determined by the *ergon*—the "characteristic activity" that defines something.

Defining this further, the characteristic activity that all human beings share in common is living in accordance with certain virtues (*aretê*) of thought and action.[1] The virtues of thought have been called "intellectual virtues"; the virtues of action have been called "moral virtues." Finally, each virtue is a mean between at least two corresponding vices.

Exploring the Ideas

The goal of *Nicomachean Ethics* is to give an account of the ultimate human good. To give an account of happiness, Aristotle asks what the characteristic activity or *ergon* of a human being is. For Aristotle, it is reason that makes a human being different from rocks, plants, and other animals, so our account of happiness must be based on the fact that people are essentially rational (reason-based) beings. Aristotle argues that the function of a human (and therefore the key to happiness) is acting in accord with the virtues (*aretê*) because virtuous activity is in accord with the rational nature of human beings.

The rational nature of human beings is a combination of practical and theoretical wisdom. Practical wisdom (*phronesis*) is a very important intellectual virtue for Aristotle's system because it makes living virtuously possible. Aristotle writes, "The mark of a man of practical wisdom [is] to be able to deliberate well about what is good and expedient for himself."[2] The practically wise person does this in two ways. First, the person is able to judge the virtuous thing to do (and how to do it) in a certain situation. Second, the presence of practical wisdom helps the virtuous person control appetites or desires that would otherwise lead them away from acting according to the moral virtues. As Aristotle emphasizes, the judgment of actions and the control of appetites through practical wisdom (*phronesis*) involves "feelings and actions" that are appropriate in certain circumstances.[3]

But one may ask why practical wisdom demands action in accord with the virtues. Aristotle suggests that practical wisdom helps us determine which character traits represent the mean between extremes of character. So, for instance, practical wisdom will show us that courage is a mean between the extremes of foolhardiness and cowardice. Foolhardiness is rushing into dangerous situations without necessity or without proper planning; cowardice is shrinking back from a dangerous situation even when an action is required to help others. So, courage—the mean between these two—is the tendency to act in order to achieve some good even when facing the risk of physical harm. Additionally, practical wisdom will help us see that although there is only one virtue to aim at in each area of human life, there may be many corresponding vices to avoid.

But what are the virtues that Aristotle associates with human happiness? Virtues are deeply ingrained character traits of thought and action, which include "moral" virtues such as justice, temperance,* generosity, friendship, and courage, as well as "intellectual" virtues such as intelligence, scientific (or certain) knowledge, and practical wisdom (*phronesis*). These virtues cannot be acquired through instruction alone but only through virtuous habits over a long period of time.

Finally, theoretical reason is another part of what separates human beings from animals. So, a thoroughly happy (or flourishing) human life is one in which the person contemplates* abstract and universal truths. The possibility of a life of philosophical activity is part of what separates us from animals and what makes us similar to the gods.[4]

So, for Aristotle, a flourishing or happy life progresses like this:

- From a young age, a person is educated well on the right kinds of habits
- By practicing these habits, the person eventually develops intellectual and moral virtues
- These intellectual and moral virtues together make the person practically wise—able to recognize and choose virtuous actions consistently and for the sake of virtue
- Finally, the happy person will have the resources necessary to act virtuously and to contemplate abstract philosophical questions. A person who leads a life of morally and intellectually virtuous activity is truly happy.

Language and Expression

The writing of *Nicomachean Ethics* is notoriously dense, probably because it was written to be given as a series of lectures to specialists in the Lyceum.* So, Aristotle's original audience would have been both well educated in philosophy and morally well educated. Furthermore, Aristotle likely would have expanded on the points he makes in the text, using illustrations and perhaps even visual aids.

The language of *Nicomachean Ethics* has had a significant impact on later moral philosophers. Three words have been very influential. First, Aristotle's use of the Greek word for happiness, *eudaimonia*, has produced a certain way of thinking about ethics.* "Eudaimonistic" ethical theories are those that focus on a rich notion of happiness or human flourishing as the goal of ethics. Another important concept that Aristotle invents is practical wisdom or practical rationality:

phronesis. Following Aristotle, most ethical theories try to account for the relationship between theoretical and practical rationality. Finally, Aristotle's insistence that some end (Greek: *telos*) is being pursued in human action has helped create the category of teleological* ethics. Teleological ethics is usually focused on discovering or describing the end toward which all human action aims, or should aim.

NOTES

1   Aristotle, *Nicomachean Ethics*, trans. Roger Crisp (Cambridge: Cambridge University Press, 2014), I.13.1103a1–10.

2   Aristotle, *Nicomachean Ethics*, VI.5.1140a25 ff.

3   Aristotle, *Nicomachean Ethics*, II.6.1106b17 ff.

4   See Aristotle, *Nicomachean Ethics*, X.7–8.

MODULE 6
SECONDARY IDEAS

KEY POINTS

- Aristotle gives a new account of why people who know the right thing to do often fail to carry it out.

- Justice and friendship, both virtues* that relate more directly to our social lives, are necessary for real flourishing.

- While allowing that good pleasures are key to a good life, Aristotle argues that pleasure cannot be the ultimate good.

Other Ideas

Some very important secondary themes in Aristotle's *Nicomachean Ethics* are voluntary action and responsibility, pleasure and pain, incontinence* (weakness of will), justice and friendship, and the virtuous person's life as a whole.

Aristotle notes that blame and praise can only be reasonably assigned to people who actually had control over what they did. Some may argue that the person who lacks virtue is too used to nonvirtuous habits to be able to choose the virtuous thing; Aristotle could respond that such a person is responsible for having chosen the actions that began the movement away from a virtuous character and toward a vicious one.

Aristotle also believes that pleasure matters for human actions: "Moral virtue is concerned with pleasures and pains; it is on account of the pleasure that we do bad things, and on account of the pain that we abstain from noble ones."[1] Pleasure tends to lead us toward bad acts and toward a lack of self-control; consequently pleasure is often not a good thing. Pleasure, however, is good when it is connected with

> ❝ Some ideas are at once so good and so convincing that it seems a pity that there is no such thing as a Nobel Prize for philosophy ... One of those bright ideas that we should be grateful to have to this very day is Aristotle's ingenious device of integrating pleasure and pain in ethical thought. ❞
>
> Dorothea Frede,* "Pleasure and Pain in Aristotle's Ethics"

virtuous activity itself. If the virtuous person sees the need to commit a courageous act of self-sacrifice, for instance, then that act is pleasant to the virtuous person.

Exploring the Ideas

In relation to his account of pleasure and pain, Aristotle also discusses the problem of a weakness of will (*akrasia*).* The problem is this: if happiness (*eudaimonia*)* is the virtuous activity that all human beings aim at, why do people fail to act virtuously—even those who seem to know what will lead to happiness? Plato* had argued that if someone does not act according to virtue, then they must suffer from a lack of knowledge. It could not be the case, according to Plato, that one could know that taking someone's property was unjust and yet still choose to take that person's property. Aristotle, however, seeks to explain the obvious truth that people often seem to know what is right and yet fail to do it; his argument is that the problem lies in the fact that such people are "incontinent"—a term he uses to describe people who lack self-restraint. Weakness of will is, for Aristotle, like a perpetual state of being "asleep, mad, or drunk."[2]

To use a modern example, although a drunken person may claim to know that that it is wrong to drive a car while drunk, it does not surprise us if the person gets behind the wheel anyway; even though drunken people use the same words as sober people, they do not genuinely understand what they are saying when they mutter, "Driving drunk is wrong." They cannot, then, really be said to *know* that it is wrong.

Similarly, an incontinent person (that is, someone who lacks self-control) is too affected by his or her desires to really know the moral claims that he or she puts forward as true. To overcome incontinence, a person must be taught to habitually choose virtuous acts. Once this person has developed the capacity to choose what is virtuous (and to do so *because* it is virtuous), the person is no longer incontinent but is virtuous.

To understand Aristotle's account of happiness, it is important to understand that his virtues were not overly individualistic or inward looking. He sees the task of moral philosophy* as continuous with political concerns. Justice and friendship are therefore important goods in Aristotle's ethical system, in that a flourishing human life will always include them. Aristotle discusses the virtue of justice in Book V and the good of friendship in Books VIII and IX. He identifies two aspects of justice—one that could be called political, and one that could be called personal. Political justice is a state of affairs that achieves the mean*—the desired middle—between one person possessing too much wealth and another person possessing too little wealth.[3] The personal aspect of justice is a personal virtue of giving people what they deserve, and it is a mean between corresponding vices. Lawless, greedy and unfair people miss the mean and are therefore unjust.[4]

Friendship, for Aristotle, comes in three kinds: friendships of utility (convenience), friendships of pleasure, and friendships of virtue.[5] While the first two are common and sometimes necessary versions of friendship, it is the last of these that is true and lasting: "Complete friendship is that of good people, those who are alike in their virtue."[6] An intriguing characteristic of Aristotle's account of justice and friendship is that, both in *Nicomachean Ethics* and in *Politics*, he suggests that the state (Greek: *polis*)* ought to play a role in developing people's character so that they come to possess the virtue of justice.

Finally, Aristotle's account of the virtues is that *eudaimonia* (happiness) really only applies to life as a whole. He does not think that a person can be said to be virtuous because of just one of his actions; on the contrary, the virtuous person can only truly be judged at the end of life, and he will possess a whole life of virtuous activity, which constitutes happiness. Aristotle states that virtue is truly present "in a complete life. For one swallow does not make a summer, nor does one day."[7] In other words, one instance of a person's fair business dealing does not make it reasonable for us to call that person just.

Overlooked

Although *Nicomachean Ethics* is one of the most highly studied philosophical texts in history, there are still some aspects that have been neglected. One area of relative neglect is the fact that Aristotle sees the great-souled person (that is, one who exhibits *megalopsuchia*)* as the highest example of virtue. A great-souled person is one who takes pride in his own generosity, who believes he is deserving of honor on a grand scale, and who is very much conscious of his own virtue and moral superiority to others. Aristotle viewed this great-souled disposition as a "sort of crown of the virtues."[8] While this account of great-souledness as the achievement of the virtues does not match the modern conception of a virtuous person, it is an important aspect of Aristotle's *Nicomachean Ethics*.

Another relatively neglected aspect of Aristotle's moral system concerns his views on the life of contemplation,* or reflection on eternal truths, and its relationship to the divine. In Book X, Aristotle returns to the question of the highest good. He argues that although action in accordance with *ethical* excellence will result in a happy life, there is something even more complete: the life of philosophical reflection. "If happiness is activity in accordance with virtue," he argues, "it is reasonable that it should be in accordance with the highest virtue ... this activity is contemplative."[9]

Aristotle's concept of a human being, then, is founded on the idea that we are essentially rational. Thus, the philosopher who contemplates mathematical and metaphysical* truths (truths about ultimate reality), as well as truths about God,[10] is said to have achieved the highest happiness and to most resemble God.

NOTES

1 Aristotle, *Nicomachean Ethics*, trans. Roger Crisp (Cambridge: Cambridge University Press, 2014), II.3.1104b9–10.

2 Aristotle, *Nicomachean Ethics*, VII.3.1147a14.

3 Aristotle, *Nicomachean Ethics*, 1133b32 ff.

4 Aristotle, *Nicomachean Ethics*, V.1.1129a32 ff.

5 Aristotle, *Nicomachean Ethics*, VIII.3.1156a6-1156b35.

6 Aristotle, *Nicomachean Ethics*, VIII.3.1156b8.

7 Aristotle, *Nicomachean Ethics*, I.7.1098a16–17.

8 Aristotle, *Nicomachean Ethics*, IV.3.1124a2.

9 J. M. Cooper, "Contemplation and Happiness: A Reconsideration," in *Reason and Emotion: Essays on Ancient Moral Psychology and Ethical Theory* (Princeton, NJ: Princeton University Press, 1999), *212*–36.

10 Aristotle, Eudemian Ethics, eds. Brad Inwood and Raphael Woolf (Cambridge: Cambridge University Press, 2013), 1249b15-25.

MODULE 7
ACHIEVEMENT

KEY POINTS

- Aristotle provides a complete and clear system of the ethical life, centered on human happiness.
- Aristotle's conception of human nature is crucial to developing his account of the virtues* that are central to happiness.
- Although the particular virtues that Aristotle identifies are derived from considering human nature, they also show a cultural influence.

Assessing The Argument

The central aim of Aristotle's *Nicomachean Ethics* is to define what a good life is. In so doing, he clarifies the notions of happiness, excellence/virtue, practical wisdom, pleasure, and friendship. He delivers a complex and detailed anthropology* (a word used here in the sense of a set of beliefs about what humans are) that has contributed to the text's enduring success. Compared with other forms of moral philosophy* of the period, *Nicomachean Ethics* stands out for its systematic and comprehensive structure and for its attempt to account for the variety of human passions and desires from a single perspective. Aristotle makes persuasive arguments against conceiving of happiness as identical to wealth, fame, or power. Similarly, he argues that because virtuous people who suffered torture had a less than happy life, virtuous character alone could not be identical to happiness. The happy person must possess virtues as well as some external goods—such as friendship and pleasure.

Aristotle also improved upon Plato's* suggestion that a person who chooses to do wrong always does so out of a lack of knowledge.

❝ Aristotle currently occupies a privileged position in the study of moral philosophy … [He] is regarded as someone whose approach to the philosophical study of ethics must be learned (though not necessarily accepted) by any serious student of the subject. More than any other philosopher from antiquity … he is read as someone whose framework for ethics might still be viable. ❞

Richard Kraut, Introduction to *The Blackwell Guide to Aristotle's Nicomachean Ethics*

Aristotle uses the concept of incontinence (here meaning weakness of will) to demonstrate that although people may have intellectual knowledge of what is right, they still may not do the right thing because of their untrained desires and passions. Aristotle's distinctive emphasis on virtuous *activity*, however, raises this question: If we are to imitate the character of the virtuous in our actions, how do we determine which people are virtuous to begin with?

Some philosophers have pointed out that if virtuous people are meant to show us which actions are right, then it seems circular (that is, a fallacy of reasoning) for Aristotle to say that we know which people are virtuous because of their right actions.

Achievement in Context

It is very difficult to determine the immediate impact of a text as ancient as *Nicomachean Ethics*, partly because there are virtually no direct quotations of *Nicomachean Ethics* outside of Aristotle's own philosophical school dating from 323 B.C.E. to 45 B.C.E.[1] By the first century B.C.E., Aristotle's ethical views seem to have been eclipsed in popularity by Stoic* ethics and Epicurean* ethics. Followers of the Stoic school of ethics famously held the view, proposed by the philosopher Socrates,* that virtue is sufficient for happiness—and not merely necessary for happiness, as Aristotle had argued; followers of the Epicurean school of ethics, on the other hand, equated happiness with pleasure. It should be noted, however, that it has been argued that *Nicomachean Ethics* did have significant influence on both Stoic and Epicurean ethics.[2]

Social and political forces played an important role in the reception of Aristotle's *Nicomachean Ethics*. For instance, before Aristotle's death in 322 B.C.E., he designated one of his followers, Theophrastus,* as his successor, and some ancient texts report that when Theophrastus in turn died in about 287 B.C.E., Aristotle's writings were taken from the students at his Lyceum* because of a condition in Theophrastus's will.[3] Aristotle's *Nicomachean Ethics*, with his other scholarly works, was not recovered until the Romans captured Athens in around 86 B.C.E.; some of his other works were unavailable in Europe until the twelfth century C.E.

Nicomachean Ethics, once recovered, played a crucial role in the development of the ethical outlook of the late Middle Ages* (the period from about the twelfth to the fifteenth centuries C.E.). For instance, in the thirteenth century, Thomas Aquinas,* the influential medieval* scholar of Christian thought, sought to integrate Aristotle's ethics with the teachings of Christian scripture. Aquinas integrated Aristotle's account of the role of the virtues of prudence, courage, justice, and practical wisdom, and also restated the supremacy of the contemplative* life, arguing that Aristotle had urged human beings to pursue a life spent contemplating God.[4]

Limitations

- Three philosophical aspects of *Nicomachean Ethics* have caused limitations in its reception—namely:
- Aristotle's argument relating to the *ergon**—function—of human beings
- His method of determining the virtues
- His culturally determined list of the virtues themselves.

The first, and most important, of these is Aristotle's notion of the objective function (*ergon*) of human beings. By this, he meant a function or purpose that exists for all people, even if they do not know it. Aristotle based his ethical system on the idea that an objective function could be discovered in human nature, thereby providing the key to human flourishing (*eudaimonia*).* This function was virtuous activity performed in accord with reason.*

The idea of human beings having a built-in function may have been readily accepted in Aristotle's Athens, but it has often been rejected by those who hold more modern, scientific world views. Indeed, one of the main objections to Aristotle's ethics also applies to his scientific thought. Aristotle had argued that things in nature have purposive (or final) causes* as well as physical causes; he argued, that is, that it is possible not only to know the physical *cause* of a change in nature, but also nature's *purpose*, or goal, in making the change. However, since the scientific revolution of the seventeenth century, science has largely restricted itself to the study of physical causes. In this light, Aristotle's views about both the function of biological* things and the function of human beings are often regarded as unscientific.

Second, many philosophers have asked how Aristotle's account can help the individual determine what to do in a certain situation. Aristotle suggests that practical wisdom (*phronesis*)* will help us know whether a certain action counts as just or unjust, courageous or cowardly. But it is only the person who already possesses the virtues to a significant extent who can be said to be practically wise. The problem here is that before one can know which virtues one ought to aim to develop, one would have to have already developed those virtues. Some philosophers have argued that this is a problematically circular argument.[5]

Finally, although Aristotle means for his list of virtues to apply to all human beings, his account turns on his specific understanding of human nature[6]—and today it is accepted that different cultures hold fundamentally different ideas of virtue.[7]

While Aristotle claims that he provides an exhaustive list of virtues,[8] his list does not contain some virtues that subsequent generations have come to value; it does not include, for example, what came to be important virtues for Christians, such as chastity or humility, nor does it contain the modern virtue of being environmentally conscious.[9] So some of the ethical substance of Aristotle's *Nicomachean Ethics* may be relevant only to a certain time and a certain group of people.

NOTES

1   Karen M. Nielsen, "The *Nicomachean Ethics* in Hellenistic Philosophy—A Hidden Treasure?" in *The Reception of Aristotle's Ethics*, ed. Jon Miller (Cambridge: Cambridge University Press, 2012), 5.

2   Nielsen, "*Nicomachean Ethics* in Hellenistic Philosophy," 5–7, 19–30.

3   Nielsen, "*Nicomachean Ethics* in Hellenistic Philosophy," 12.

4   Ralph McInerny and John O'Callaghan, "Saint Thomas Aquinas," in *Stanford Encyclopedia of Philosophy*, ed. Edward N. Zalta, (May 23, 2014 edn.), accessed December 10, 2015, http://plato.stanford.edu/entries/aquinas/#ThoAri.

5   See, for instance, J. L. Mackie, *Ethics: Inventing Right and Wrong* (London: Penguin, 1977), 186.

6   Aristotle, *Nicomachean Ethics*, trans. David Ross, in The Complete Works of Aristotle, ed. J. Barnes (Princeton, NJ: Princeton University Press, 1991), I.7.1097b22–1098a20.

7   The excellences of character—which we could call "moral virtues"—are discussed in Aristotle, *Nicomachean Ethics*, III.6–V.11.

8   Aristotle, *Nicomachean Ethics*, III.6.1115a5 and IV.7.1127a16-17.

9   Rosalind Hursthouse, "Virtue Ethics," section 2, in *Stanford Encyclopedia of Philosophy*, ed. Edward N. Zalta, (Fall 2013 edn.), accessed February 27, 2016, http://plato.stanford.edu/archives/fall2013/entries/ethics-virtue/.

MODULE 8
PLACE IN THE AUTHOR'S LIFE AND WORK

KEY POINTS

- Aristotle wrote on the philosophical* aspects of almost everything there was to know in his time (natural science, psychology, mathematics, rhetoric,* politics), and even invented new sciences such as logic* and biology.*

- Based on an earlier lecture course on ethics,* *Nicomachean Ethics* is a mature work that relies on many of Aristotle's other works.

- The product of extensive research, *Nicomachean Ethics* is one of Aristotle's greatest works; it continues to be seen as a high point in the Aristotelian corpus* (body of work).

Positioning

Aristotle most likely wrote *Nicomachean Ethics* during his most productive time, his second stay in Athens, from 335 to 323 B.C.E., the period in which he composed the majority of his works. Most of the works handed down to us from this period are written roughly, in the form of lecture notes or seminar papers for his school, the Lyceum.* *Nicomachean Ethics* is not the only ethical treatise under Aristotle's name. He also wrote the earlier *Eudemian Ethics* (probably named after one of his students). *Magna Moralia* has also been attributed to Aristotle, but most scholars believe that while this text has key Aristotelian ideas, he probably did not draft it himself.[1]

The relationship between *Nicomachean* and *Eudemian Ethics* is hard to determine—an issue complicated by the fact that the two works share about a third of their content. One modern Aristotle scholar

> **❝** The Corpus of Aristotle's works contains two treatises bearing the name *Ethics—the Nicomachean and the Eudemian* ... The [Nicomachean] should probably be assigned to the latest period of Aristotle's life, the period of his headship of the Lyceum, i.e. to his fifties or sixties. **❞**
>
> David Ross, *The Nicomachean Ethics of Aristotle*

from the United States, Chris Bobonich,* argues, "The more common scholarly opinion is that *Nicomachean Ethics* is the later work, and it has been regarded as Aristotle's major and definitive work on ethics at least since the first or second century [B.C.E.]."[2] Most interpreters agree that *Nicomachean Ethics* is more important than *Eudemian Ethics*, and it is viewed by scholars as the culmination of Aristotle's thinking on moral matters. This is shown by the fact that it draws on almost every other part of his philosophy, such as logic, his thoughts on the human soul, metaphysics* (the branch of philosophy dealing with fundamental questions such as what exists and what is the nature of reality), and his political philosophy. *Politics* starts at the end of *Nicomachean Ethics*, at the end of the tenth book, and the two works are conceived of as a unitary whole.

Integration

Aristotle's output as a writer is impressive: ancient catalogues credit him with the authorship of more than 150 books.[3] Many of these works, in particular the popular dialogues, are lost. Only about 2,450 pages in English translation have survived from antiquity. Moreover, Aristotle's body of work was edited to its present state by Andronicus of Rhodes,* a scholar who was probably the leader of the Lyceum in the first century B.C.E. It was Andronicus who originated the famous philosophical word "metaphysics" (literally "after physics") because he placed Aristotle's book by that name after his book on physics. The surviving texts tend to have an unfinished feel, which leads scholars to think they are either lecture notes that Aristotle revised and rewrote over time or notes taken by one of his students during lectures.

Since ancient times, the corpus has been divided into five distinct areas, according to content rather than the order in which they were written. These are:

- Works dealing with logic, known as the *Organon* (the "instrument"), a highly influential set of texts used through the Middle Ages* to teach logic and debate
- Aristotle's landmark works on nature and biology
- *Metaphysics,* an investigation concerning the ultimate nature of reality
- The study of human action, including the two treatises* on ethics—*Nicomachean Ethics* and *Eudemian Ethics*—as well as *Politics*
- A work on the theory of tragedy and the famous *Rhetoric*.[4]

The most important connection between Aristotle's ethical and political works and his other works is arguably the relationship they bear to his biological theories. While Aristotle spent much time detailing and categorizing species, he also seems to have thought that biological species had certain functions or purposes—an attitude paralleled in Aristotle's understanding of human nature. For Aristotle, there was a certain set of functions that set human beings apart from other animals and thereby gave insight into how we ought to act and live.

Significance

The importance of *Nicomachean Ethics* and of Aristotle's body of work in general is difficult to overestimate. The American professor Ron Polansky* writes, "Aristotle's *Nicomachean Ethics* is among the first systematic treatments of ethics, and it is arguably the most important and influential philosophical work ever devoted to its field. With glorious preparation in the thought of Socrates* and Plato,* and equipped with a rigorous depth in all the principal areas of inquiry, Aristotle aimed for a comprehensive presentation of ethics that could stand the test of time."[5]

The many who follow his philosophy more closely are called Aristotelians, or Peripatetics,* after the circular walkway (*peripatos*) that stood next to the Lyceum.

The philosophy of Aristotle was extremely influential during the late Middle Ages (around 1200–1500 C.E.). During this time, Aristotle was simply called "The Philosopher," and his works represented the most highly regarded wisdom about the world. Great thinkers, such as the Italian astronomer Galileo Galilei,* the French philosopher René Descartes,* and the Polish astronomer Nicolaus Copernicus,* started to move away from Aristotle's theories about nature in the sixteenth and seventeenth centuries, especially in physics and astronomy. Additionally, moral philosophers,* such as David Hume* and Immanuel Kant,* moved away from Aristotle in the eighteenth century. Despite this historical change, *Nicomachean Ethics* maintained its importance as a classic in moral philosophy.

There is a vast literature on Aristotle, and on *Nicomachean Ethics* in particular. The work has also played a significant role in contemporary moral philosophy. The recent "virtue ethics"* movement, which focuses on moral character as the basis for ethics, is inspired by Aristotle's emphasis on virtue in moral conduct. Famous modern moral philosophers, such as the English virtue ethicist Philippa Foot,* the Scottish thinker Alasdair MacIntyre,* and the US scholar Martha Nussbaum,* are followers of Aristotle.[6]

NOTES

1   For an argument in favor of the authenticity of the *Magna Moralia* see J. M. Cooper, "The *Magna Moralia* and Aristotle's Moral Philosophy," *American Journal of Philology (*1973): 327–49. Against it argues C. Rowe, "A Reply to John Cooper on the *Magna Moralia*," *American Journal of Philology (*1975): 160–72.

2   Aristotle, *Nicomachean Ethics*, trans. David Ross, in *The Complete Works of Aristotle*, ed. J. Barnes (Princeton, NJ: Princeton University Press, 1991), viii; and Chris Bobonich, "Aristotle's Ethical Treatises," in *The Blackwell Guide to Aristotle's Nicomachean Ethics*, ed. Richard Kraut (London: Wiley-Blackwell, 2006), 12–36. The most trenchant critique of the standard view is offered by Anthony Kenny, *The Aristotelian Ethics: A Study of the Relationship Between the* Eudemian *and* Nicomachean Ethics *of Aristotle* (Oxford: *Clarendon Press,* 1978).

3   Diogenes Laertius V.21 ff., in Diogenes Laertius, *Lives of Eminent Philosophers*, ed. R. D. Hicks (Cambridge, MA: *Harvard University Press,* 1966).

4   All works are found in Barnes, *Complete Works of Aristotle*.

5   R. Polansky, "Introduction: Ethics as Practical Science," in *The Cambridge Companion to Aristotle's Nicomachean Ethics*, ed. R. Polansky (Cambridge: Cambridge University Press, 2014), 1.

6   M. C. Nussbaum, "Non-Relative Virtues: An Aristotelian Approach," in *The Quality of Life*, eds. M. C. Nussbaum and A. Sen (Oxford: Clarendon Press, 1993), 242–69.

SECTION 3
IMPACT

THE FIRST RESPONSES

KEY POINTS

- It is likely that *Nicomachean Ethics* resulted from the revision of Aristotle's earlier *Eudemian Ethics*.

- It is impossible to form a complete critical history of Aristotle's *Nicomachean Ethics* starting at the time it was written.

- Stoicism,* Epicureanism,* and Skepticism,* approaches to virtuous behavior founded by Aristotle's contemporaries, were the competing moral systems in the centuries after *Nicomachean Ethics* was published.

Criticism

It is not easy to assess the immediate influence, positive or negative, of Aristotle's *Nicomachean Ethics*. Unlike Plato's* influential work on government in *Republic*—which sparked responses from quite a few of its ancient Greek and Roman readers—*Nicomachean Ethics* does not seem to have been published. There is no reference to it in any surviving text until the first century B.C.E., when a reference is found in *De Finibus* (*On Ends*) by Cicero (106–43 B.C.E.). This indicates that it was probably not circulated outside of Aristotle's school, the Lyceum,* during his lifetime or for some time after his death in 322 B.C.E. This would explain why there are no direct criticisms of *Nicomachean Ethics*, and no responses by Aristotle to these criticisms.

Nevertheless, the Aristotelian position was sufficiently well known that it was probably considered, if not by name then at least in spirit, by all the major Hellenistic* schools: the Stoics, the Epicureans, and the Skeptics. (The Hellenistic period—from Hellas, the Greek name for

❝ Writing the reception history of the *Nicomachean Ethics* in Hellenistic philosophy is, arguably, an impossible task. The problem is not simply the paucity of evidence. We have no direct citations tying any doctrine discussed by Epicurean, Stoic, or Academic [that is, adherents of the form of skepticism about ethical knowledge which came about in Plato's Academy] philosophers to views explicitly defended by Aristotle in the [*Nicomachean Ethics*]. ❞

Karen M. Nielsen, "*The Nicomachean Ethics* in Hellenistic Philosophy"

the territory—lasted from the death of Alexander the Great* in 323 B.C.E. to the beginning of the Roman Empire in 31 B.C.E.) The Stoics did not accept Aristotle's view that external goods are necessary for happiness, and instead held to the Socratic* view that virtue is sufficient to achieve happiness. The Epicureans equated happiness with moderate pleasure, rather than with the activity of a rational soul, while the Skeptics disagreed with Aristotle's claim that we can really know what virtue is, claiming that philosophical* reflection will not assist us in discovering or achieving it.

Responses

In the history of moral philosophy,* Professor Terence Irwin* has said that "we can follow one significant thread through the history of moral philosophy by considering how far Aristotle is right, and what his successors think about his claims."[1] Regarding the first responses, however, this assessment is difficult to make since we have little or no direct evidence of the responses to Aristotle's *Nicomachean Ethics* during his lifetime.

We do, however, know that defenders of Aristotle's ethical system existed later in the ancient world. Alexander of Aphrodisias* of the late second and early third century c.e., for example, argues against the Stoics' view that the faultless exercise of virtue is all one could desire. For him, the virtuous person also wants his or her action to achieve its purpose. According to Stoic thought, it does not matter whether the money one gives to charity really reaches the people in need: if one has acted virtuously, and the money is misused through no fault of one's own, then one's action is as good as it could be. Alexander, however, defends what he takes to be Aristotle's view, as Aristotle emphasizes that reaching the goal is important for morally good action.[2] Aristotle did not, then, himself do battle with his critics; instead, his followers fought for him. This is a recurring—and continuing—pattern in the history of Aristotelian philosophy.

Conflict and Consensus

While there is no direct historical evidence of Aristotle receiving criticism of his ethical views and changing them in response, this must largely be on account of the historical distance between Aristotle and readers today. It would surely be wrong to assume that Aristotle did not take criticism at the time into account, and that no critical interaction with his ethical thought took place. On the contrary, since Aristotle was at one point a student at Plato's Academy* and at another point the head of the philosophical school called the Lyceum, it is likely that he received feedback and criticism of his views over the course of his philosophical career.

Furthermore, most scholars attribute the authorship of two ethical treatises* to Aristotle: *Nicomachean Ethics* and *Eudemian Ethics*.[3] It is significant, however, that although the two works have three books in common (*Nicomachean Ethics* V–VII and *Eudemian Ethics* IV–VI), there are important ethical concepts that differ between the two. For instance, Aristotle's concept of practical wisdom (*phronesis*)* is not consistent over the two works. In *Eudemian Ethics*, it is a more abstract, theoretical faculty (similar to what Plato termed *sophia**—wisdom); in

Nicomachean Ethics, it is exclusively practical.[4] Since the division of the sciences between theoretical, practical, and productive activities is Aristotle's final position, it would seem that Aristotle wrote *Nicomachean Ethics* after *Eudemian Ethics*—likely after a revision of some of his ethical concepts. Such an account also aligns with the fact that Aristotle increasingly moved away from Plato's philosophical position over the course of his life. This theory is based on the nature of the texts themselves, however, rather than on external evidence.

NOTES

1   T. Irwin, *The Development of Ethics*, Vol. 1 (Oxford: Oxford University Press, 2007), 4.

2   Aristotle, *Nicomachean Ethics*, rev. ed., trans. Roger Crisp (Cambridge: Cambridge University Press, 2014), X.7.1177b16–26.

3   "Introduction" by Roger Crisp, in Aristotle, *Nicomachean Ethics*, vii–viii.

4   Frederick Copleston, *A History of Philosophy: Greece and Rome* (London: Continuum Press, 2003), 270.

MODULE 10
THE EVOLVING DEBATE

KEY POINTS

* Aristotle's systematic exploration of virtue* greatly influenced Christian and non-Christian approaches to virtue.

* Aristotle's philosophy as a whole, including ethics,* was continued after his death by his followers, called the Peripatetics,* and, more critically, by followers of Plato.*

* The medieval* Christian scholar Thomas Aquinas's* interpretation of Aristotle's ethics, which sees human nature as the key for virtue and good action, continues to be explored by neo-Aristotelians*—that is, scholars who draw on Aristotle's ideas—today.

Uses And Problems

Although Aristotle's *Nicomachean Ethics*, completed between 335 and 323 B.C.E., has proved one of the most influential works in the history of philosophy, its popularity and influence have varied over time. During the period immediately after Aristotle's death, the development of his ethics apparently took place primarily within his school, the Lyceum.* The members of this school are known as the Peripatetics. Aristotle's system was eclipsed during the Hellenistic* (322–31 B.C.E.) and Roman* (27 B.C.E.–395 C.E.) periods by Stoic* ethics and Epicureanism*—different approaches to the definition of the well-lived life.

Epicureanism was a school founded by the Greek philosopher Epicurus* (341–270 B.C.E.), who argued that happiness consists of pleasure (Greek: *hedone*).* Epicurus, however, defines pleasure as "freedom from bodily pain and mental anguish," and he believed that

> ❝ Aquinas has at least three aims in his moral philosophy: 1) He tries to say what Aristotle means, and what an Aristotelian conception of morality commits us to. 2) He tries to show that this conception of morality is defensible on philosophical grounds. 3) He seeks to show that it also satisfies the theological and moral demands of Christian doctrine. ❞
>
> Terence Irwin, *The Development of Ethics*

virtues (such as justice and temperance)* protect one from the psychological distress caused by indiscriminate pleasure seeking[1]—a view incompatible with that of Aristotle. For Aristotle, virtuous activity *is* happiness, and pleasure coincides with it; for Epicurus, pleasure *is* happiness and virtue is the way to attain pleasure. Though there is no direct evidence for an influence of Aristotle upon Epicureanism, some scholars believe that since the key categories are the same, Aristotle had an influence on Epicureanism.[2]

The Stoics, following Socrates* and Plato, held that virtuous character is sufficient for happiness. While this contradicted Aristotle's theory about happiness, many scholars maintain that Aristotle nonetheless had an impact on Stoic ethical concepts. An example of this influence is the Stoic emphasis on actions "according to nature"— an idea similar to Aristotle's emphasis on determining ethics through the study of human nature.[3] So, it is reasonable to see both Epicureanism and Stoicism as in some ways evolving from Aristotle's ethical categories.

Aristotle's ethics were embraced extensively during the Christian Middle Ages* (the fifth to the fifteenth centuries C.E.), when many philosophers and religious scholars (among them Albertus Magnus* and Thomas Aquinas in the thirteenth century) wrote commentaries on *Nicomachean Ethics*.[4] Later philosophers continued this attention during the Renaissance,* the period of the fourteenth to the seventeenth centuries during which European culture was reinvigorated by a turn toward classical models. The philosopher Francisco Suarez,* for instance, agrees with Aristotle that human nature has universal purposes that form the basis for ethics.

Later philosophers, however, increasingly disagreed with the medieval linkage between Aristotelian and Christian ethics. The British philosopher Thomas Hobbes* (1588–1679 C.E.), for example, argued that physical causes are responsible for all human behavior, rather than final or purposive causes* (that is, the goals or purposes of a person's behavior). Hobbes' view—that human actions resemble the workings of a machine rather than being the result of a person exercising free will—became more dominant in modern philosophy.[5] There was therefore a decline in the popularity of Aristotelian ethics as a complete system in the centuries following the Middle Ages. Around the middle of the twentieth century, however, many philosophers returned to Aristotle as an enlightening moral philosopher for the contemporary world.

Schools of Thought

Perhaps the most important school of thought established by Aristotle's ethics is the medieval Scholastic* tradition. Within this tradition, medieval scholars translated and critically interpreted the writings of Plato, Aristotle, and the Bible. In this process, they sought to combine all these sources of moral and philosophical authority. Such commentaries include the *Super Ethica*—the philosopher Albertus Magnus's commentary on Aristotle's *Nicomachean Ethics*. The book was completed in about 1250 C.E. and became arguably the most influential book on ethics written in the Middle Ages.[6] Also important was Thomas Aquinas's commentary, a work completed in the early 1270s C.E. Most importantly, Aquinas combined Aristotle's ethical system into his extremely influential masterwork, *Summa Theologiae* (written from 1265 to 1274). Aquinas, following Aristotle, maintains that each virtue is a mean* (or desired middle) between vices, and holds that practical reason (in Aquinas's Latin, *prudentia*) is the source of our knowledge concerning which actions and character traits are indeed virtuous.[7]

Indeed, Terence Irwin* argues that Aquinas attempted to build a philosophical defense of Aristotle's ethics and to combine it with Christian thought. Aquinas was respectful of Aristotle, and Irwin describes how he was deeply affected by Aristotle's moral theory. It should be noted here, however, that many scholars argue that Aquinas contributed his own philosophical reflection, which improved upon Aristotle's ethics.[8] Even so, because of the influence that Aquinas's work had upon subsequent Christian theologians, Aristotle can be said to have exercised an influence upon the intellectual and ethical outlook of the Middle Ages.

In Current Scholarship

The past 60 years or so have seen renewed interest in the relevance of Aristotle's ethics to both academic philosophy and the modern world. As evidence of this, recent years have seen two entire anthologies devoted to *Nicomachean Ethics*. These are *The Cambridge Companion to Aristotle's* Nicomachean Ethics, and *Aquinas and the* Nicomachean Ethics.[9] The second work demonstrates Aristotle's influence through other traditions, from the Middle Ages to the twenty-first century. This latest renewal of interest in *Nicomachean Ethics* began with the British philosopher Elizabeth Anscombe's* 1958 article "Modern Moral Philosophy,"[10] which called for a reexamination of Aristotle's ethics in light of moral philosophers' confused use of the notion of "moral obligation" in twentieth-century moral theory. Such an examination, said Anscombe, would push us to seek a clear definition of "a virtue," and might bring with it fresh insights into ethics.

Many moral philosophers have since sought to develop an essentially Aristotelian account of ethics; two of the most prominent are the Scottish philosopher Alasdair MacIntyre* and the philosopher Rosalind Hursthouse* of New Zealand. MacIntyre wrote the highly influential book *After Virtue* (1981), in which he argues that the contemporary world is characterized by incoherence and unending disagreement about ethics, stemming from a modern rejection of Aristotle's belief in the intrinsic purposes of human nature.[11] A more consistent approach, MacIntyre argues, will only be recovered as some form of Aristotle's ethics.

Similarly, Hursthouse argues in her *On Virtue Ethics* (2001) that it is a mistake to think of virtue ethics* as focused only on the character of the individual. Rather, virtue ethics is able to provide concrete guidance about the appropriate norms or principles of behavior. Hursthouse's account provides rules related to virtues and vices. As she states, "Not only does each virtue generate a prescription—do what is honest, charitable, generous—but each vice a prohibition—do not do what is dishonest, uncharitable, mean."[12] Hursthouse follows Aristotle's *Nicomachean Ethics* in both her emphasis on the virtues and her insistence that virtuous *action* is the aim of her theory.

NOTES

1   Quoted from Diogenes Laertius, *Lives of Eminent Philosophers*, ed. R. D. Hicks (Cambridge, MA: *Harvard University Press,* 1966), X.129–32; also quoted in M. Andrew Holowchak, Happiness and Greek Ethical Thought (London: Continuum Press, 2005), 76.

2   See Karen M. Nielsen, "The *Nicomachean Ethics* in Hellenistic Philosophy: A Hidden Treasure?" in *The Reception of Aristotle's Ethics*, ed. Jon Miller (Cambridge: Cambridge University Press, 2012), 6–8.

3   Nielsen, "*Nicomachean Ethics* in Hellenistic Philosophy," 6; and A. A. Long, "Aristotle's Legacy to Stoic Ethics," *Bulletin of the Institute of Classical Study* 15, no. 1 (1968): 72–85.

4   Anthony Celano, "The Relation of Prudence and *Synderesis* to Happiness in the Medieval Commentaries on Aristotle's Ethics," in Miller, *The Reception of Aristotle's Ethics*, 125–54.

5   See Donald Rutherford, "The End of Ends? Aristotelian Themes in Early Modern Ethics," in Miller, *Reception of Aristotle's Ethics*, 194–221.

6   Celano, "Relation of Prudence and *Synderesis* to Happiness," 138; see also R. A. Gauthier "Trois commentaries 'averroistes' sur l'Ethique a Nicomaque," *Archives d'histoire doctrinale et litteraire du moyen age* 16, no. 1 (1947–8): 187–336.

7   Jennifer A. Herdt, "Aquinas's Aristotelian Defense of Martyr Courage," in *Aquinas and the* Nicomachean Ethics, eds. Tobias Hoffman, Jorn Muller and Matthias Perkams (Cambridge: Cambridge University Press, 2013), 125; cf. John Finnis, "Aquinas's Moral, Political, and Legal Philosophy," in *Stanford Encyclopedia of Philosophy*, ed. by Edward N. Zalta (Summer 2014 edn.), accessed January 15, 2016, http://plato.stanford.edu/archives/sum2014/entries/aquinas-moral-political/.

8   For an account of this ethical system, as well as Aquinas's divergences from Aristotle, see Finnis, "Aquinas's Moral, Political, and Legal Philosophy".

9   See R. Polansky (ed.), *The Cambridge Companion to Aristotle's* Nicomachean Ethics (Cambridge: Cambridge University Press, 2014); and Tobias Hoffman, Jörn Muller and Matthias Perkams (eds.), *Aquinas and the* Nicomachean Ethics (Cambridge: Cambridge University Press, 2013).

10 G. E. M. Anscombe, "Modern Moral Philosophy," *Philosophy* 33, no. 124 (1958): 1–19.

11 See Alasdair MacIntyre, *After Virtue*, 3rd edn. (Notre Dame: University of Notre Dame Press, 2007), 1–3, 109–20.

12 Rosalind Hursthouse, *On Virtue Ethics* (Oxford: Oxford University Press, 2001), 36.

MODULE 11
IMPACT AND INFLUENCE TODAY

KEY POINTS

- *Nicomachean Ethics* is a key text for the development of contemporary virtue ethics.*

- Those critical of virtue ethics complain that virtue* does not give you a sufficient set of rules to guide action—it tells you to act well, but not what to do.

- Virtue ethicists deny that an ethical system can specify a straightforward rule for what to do in any given situation, so that practical wisdom (*phronesis*)* is a necessary part of an adequate moral philosophy.*

Position

The ideas put forward in Aristotle's *Nicomachean Ethics* are key to understanding the history of moral philosophy. However, between the beginning of the nineteenth century and the 1950s, Aristotle's approach was not viewed as a practical philosophical option. In 1958, the British philosopher Elizabeth Anscombe* challenged this in a highly influential article on modern moral philosophy.[1] She contrasted modern moral philosophers with Aristotle, arguing that they failed to give a coherent account of the meaning of "moral ought" and "moral obligation."[2] She noted, however, that Aristotle maintained a coherent ethical system without using such problematic terms; rather, Aristotle focused on richer concepts such as "justice" and "courage." So, a return to his ethics could provide a way forward in understanding morality through developing an updated account of the virtues. This text helped launch the neo-Aristotelian* movement—a school of modern thinkers whose work centers on virtue ethics.

> ❝ The particular version of virtue ethics I detail in the book is ... known as 'neo-Aristotelian.' The general kind is 'neo' for at least the reason ... that its proponents allow themselves to regard Aristotle as just plain wrong on slaves and women. ... It is 'Aristotelian' insofar as it aims to stick pretty close to his ethical writings wherever else it can. ❞
>
> Rosalind Hursthouse, *On Virtue Ethics*

In the 1980s, Alasdair MacIntyre's* *After Virtue* (1981) discussed the nature of a virtue; this was an updated version of Aristotle's argument regarding function (*ergon*).* In *After Virtue*, MacIntyre argues that the function of human beings is determined by the nature of the roles they fill in a society, rather than by universal biological purpose, as Aristotle had suggested. According to MacIntyre, the virtues are those well-formed character traits necessary for excellence within different practices and social roles.

Finally, the New Zealand philosopher Rosalind Hursthouse's* *On Virtue Ethics* (2001) sought to revive Aristotle's views on virtues, arguing that they provide guidance on how people should act in certain situations, while vices offer guidance on avoiding certain actions. These examples show that over the past 60 years there has been a revival of Aristotle's ideas.

Interaction

The current revival of Aristotle's *Nicomachean Ethics* represents a challenge to the major ethical theories of our day—consequentialism* and Kantian* ethics.* Consequentialism states that the goodness of an action or an intention or an emotion is determined by its consequences alone; Kantian ethics states that an action is right if, and only if, it is an expression of a rule that could (with consistency) be made a universal law for all rational beings.[3]

For the first half of the twentieth century, Aristotle's *Nicomachean Ethics* seemed irrelevant in comparison with these two systems of ethics. However, because of Anscombe's highly influential criticisms of modern moral philosophy, Aristotle's work has more recently received greater attention.[4]

The philosophers grouped as neo-Aristotelians have criticized consequentialism and Kantian ethics in several ways.

First, they have pointed out that the development of character is important in moral education and ethical reflection. An approach—such as Aristotle's—that stresses the development of the virtues reflects our actual moral development more than an account that only produces rules for what actions to avoid or carry out.

Second, virtue ethicists have emphasized the important relationship between emotions and the moral life.[5] A rationalistic* approach, such as Kantian ethics, founded on the assumption that knowledge must be derived from theoretical reason, often fails to appreciate how much people rely on their emotions in deciding what is the right action. As Hursthouse argues, "there is indeed much in Kant" to suggest that his account "makes the emotions no part of our rational nature."[6] Her emphasis on combining emotion with practical rationality is a development of Aristotle's view that practical rationality must govern both our feelings *and* our actions; as Aristotle says, "virtue is to do with feelings and actions."[7]

Finally, virtue ethicists argue that other ethical theories, such as consequentialism, rely on problematic ideas of human nature or basic values. For instance, utilitarianism,* a form of consequentialism, relies on the assumption that we should maximize pleasure and reduce pain in all our actions. As Aristotle pointed out, however, "pleasure" is often a confused concept.[8] Sometimes it stands for some psychological state; at other times, it stands for a certain kind of activity.[9] Accordingly, we can speak of pleasure as the positive psychological side effect of something we like or we can say things like "playing soccer is my favorite pleasure." On the basis of Aristotle's insights about the ambiguous ways we talk about pleasure, Anscombe argues that utilitarians "do not notice the difficulty with the concept of pleasure."[10]

This notion of pleasure, then, cannot be the basis for ethics in its entirety. As a result of these arguments from virtue ethicists, many proponents of consequentialist and Kantian ethics have sought to provide an account of the role of the virtues and moral development from within their own systems.[11]

The Continuing Debate

As stated above, Kantianism bases the rightness of actions on whether people are acting according to an appropriate rule, and consequentialism holds that the rightness of an action depends solely on expected outcomes. Supporters of these theories have highlighted several objections to virtue ethics generally and to Aristotle's ethics particularly.

First of all, virtue ethics, especially as Aristotle presents it in *Nicomachean Ethics*, seems to fall short of providing us with actual ethical guidance. Aristotle and his followers maintain that the highest good for human beings is acting in accord with the virtues. But Aristotle also thinks we develop moral character by habits in our early moral education, and without this moral education, we cannot become the kind of people who recognize the goodness of the life of virtue—a person must have good character before he can recognize what it takes to develop the virtues. As the philosopher J. L. Mackie* concludes, "this is too circular to be very helpful."[12]

Some moral philosophers object to Aristotle's ethics because his list of virtues is based on the culture in which he lived, rather than on enduring, universal truth. As the British moral philosopher Bernard Williams* summarizes, "there is a question to be discussed about the extent of the distance we should acknowledge between Aristotle's conceptions and styles of ethical thought and styles of ethical thought we might find acceptable now."[13] Thus, Aristotelians face the task of explaining that while virtues apparently change over time, ethical truth does not.

Most would now argue, for example, that Aristotle's exclusion of women (and all people without property) from the possibility of virtue is a significant cultural blind spot. The moral philosopher Martha Nussbaum* pushes back on the charge that Aristotle simply reflects his culture's values, however, writing, "If we probe further into the way in which Aristotle in fact [numbers and distinguishes] the virtues, we begin to notice things that cast doubt upon the suggestion that he simply described what was admired in his own society."[14] While Aristotle was influenced by his own Athenian context, he sought to both defend its best aspects and criticize what was lacking. So, while one might admit that Aristotle's list of the virtues is not perfect or universal, this is not necessarily a reason to abandon his basic approach to the ethical life. One simply needs to be open to revising one's list of the virtues if someone else has a better list.[15]

NOTES

1   G. E. M. Anscombe, "Modern Moral Philosophy," *Philosophy* 33, no. 124 (1958).

2   Anscombe, "Modern Moral Philosophy," 4–5.

3   For a version of Kantian ethics, see Christine Korsgaard, *Sources of Normativity* (Cambridge: Cambridge University Press, 2012), 19–20.

4   Anscombe, "Modern Moral Philosophy."

5   Aristotle, *Nicomachean Ethics*, trans. Roger Crisp (Cambridge: Cambridge University Press, 2014), I.8.1099a7–21; II.6.1106b16–17.

6   Rosalind Hursthouse, *On Virtue Ethics* (Oxford: Oxford University Press, 2001), 109.

7   Aristotle, *Nicomachean Ethics*, III.1,1109b.30; cf. II.5, 1105b.20 ff.

8   Aristotle, *Nicomachean Ethics*, X.5, 1175a, 23 ff.

9   See G. E. M. Anscombe, "Modern Moral Philosophy;" and Alasdair
     MacIntyre, *After Virtue* (Notre Dame: University of Notre Dame Press, 2007),
     62–4.

10 Anscombe, "Modern Moral Philosophy," 2.

11 For an account of the virtues in David Hume and Immanuel Kant's moral
     philosophies, see Martha Nussbaum, "Virtue Ethics: A Misleading
     Category?" *Journal of Ethics* 3, no. 3 (1999): 163–201.

12 J. L. Mackie, *Ethics: Inventing Right and Wrong* (London: Penguin, 1977),
     186.

13 Bernard Williams, *Ethics and the Limits of Philosophy* (London: Routledge,
     2006), 49.

14 Martha Nussbaum, "Non-Relative Virtues: An Aristotelian Approach,"
     Midwest Studies in Philosophy 13, no. 1 (1998): 34.

15 For an example of this approach, see Alasdair MacIntyre's *Whose Justice?
     Which Rationality?* (London: Duckworth, 1988), especially "The Rationality
     of Traditions," 349–69.

MODULE 12
WHERE NEXT?

KEY POINTS

- *Nicomachean Ethics* will continue to be one of the most influential treatises* on ethics.*

- As the classic text on virtue ethics,* supporters and opponents of virtue ethics will continue to refer to Aristotle's *Nicomachean Ethics*; discussion will continue to return to it.

- *Nicomachean Ethics* provides a comprehensive ethical system of virtue essential to many ethical systems that center on virtue.

Potential

The potential of Aristotle's *Nicomachean Ethics* to influence contemporary and future philosophy* is mainly linked to the fortunes of virtue ethics.[1] Virtue ethicists take their inspiration and key themes from *Nicomachean Ethics*, highlighting topics such as virtue, happiness, and practical wisdom. As Rosalind Hursthouse* writes, "Virtue ethics is both an old and a new approach to ethics, old in so far as it dates back to the writings of Plato* and, more particularly, Aristotle, new in that, as a revival of this ancient approach, it is a fairly recent addition to contemporary moral theory."[2]

There is now sustained philosophical interest in the question of whether virtue ethics really does provide a useful alternative to standard moral theories, and whether Aristotle's version of virtue ethics is the best one.

Furthermore, there is an effort to expand upon Aristotle's *Nicomachean Ethics*, making its framework relevant even to issues he

> ❝ While it is possible that Aristotle does not, after all, have a virtue ethics, the realization of this possibility is at odds with the expressly neo-Aristotelian character of much virtue ethics, so nicely expressed by Ruth Anna Putnam's ostensive definition of virtue ethics: '... virtue ethics is what Aristotle did.' ❞
>
> Sean McAleer, "An Aristotelian Account of Virtue Ethics"

did not speak to directly. The Aristotle scholar Sarah Broadie* believes that Aristotelians must be careful in this area. In spite of the fact that "much of what [Aristotle] *does* have to say in *Nicomachean Ethics* continues to shape our own thinking," she writes, we tend to overlook the equally important fact that "many of our own central preoccupations in ethics are with questions on which, for one or another reason, Aristotle has little or nothing to say."[3] In these cases, some virtue ethicists give an answer that they take to be in the Aristotelian spirit. This, in turn, prompts scholars to look at the text afresh, with the concerns of modern virtue ethicists in mind.

Future Directions

The rise of virtue ethics is also responsible for the further development of core aspects of *Nicomachean Ethics*, although not all virtue ethicists are neo-Aristotelians.* Although many virtue ethicists agree with Aristotle's central argument that a good life consists of virtuous activity,[4] some aspects of the text need to be updated, seeming to be tailored for a certain society at a certain time—namely, Athens in the fourth century B.C.E. Thus, Aristotle's virtues are not necessarily our virtues (and vice versa);[5] Aristotle has no virtue that would cover our interaction with the environment, for example. In the future, virtue ethics will continue to provide fruitful discussions of questions about abortion (termination of pregnancy), euthanasia (mercy killing), and medical research from a virtue ethics perspective.[6]

Since virtue plays such an important role in ethical development, educators have begun to focus again more on the development of character. This insight goes back to a concern voiced by Aristotle in the text's final book: that moral education must begin at a young age.[7] Some educators have argued that one should explain to the child the relevant virtue and vice in a given situation, and discourage or encourage the child in terms of virtue and vice.[8] Even if Aristotle does not cover all of our practical concerns, *Nicomachean Ethics* is still relevant, and provides a useful framework within which to develop virtues for our society and time. The Aristotle scholar Paula Gottlieb* remarks, "No doubt in all Aristotle's ethical works there are gems waiting to be discovered and fruitful new lines of enquiry to be pursued, even after two thousand years of study."[9]

Summary

Aristotle's *Nicomachean Ethics* is an ancient, well-organized, highly original, and groundbreaking discussion of ethical theory. Its central argument is that the human good consists of activity—action—in accord with the moral and intellectual virtues. Aristotle ties in almost all of the elements that we still find important in ethical theory: moral character and its acquisition; human action; emotion; pleasure; and the virtues. Hursthouse has summarized the influence of Aristotle's ethics as follows, "Virtue ethics' founding fathers are Plato* and, more particularly, Aristotle ... and it persisted as the dominant approach in Western moral philosophy* until at least the Enlightenment.* It suffered a momentary eclipse during the nineteenth century but re-emerged in the late 1950s in Anglo-American philosophy."[10]

In short, Aristotle's *Nicomachean Ethics* has had a profound impact on the study of philosophy.

The contemporary re-emergence of Aristotle's ethics has had a widespread impact upon moral philosophy, and there are signs that this influence will continue. *Nicomachean Ethics* still has few rivals even among the most influential works of its period dealing with ethics. But this influence is not merely academic. Aristotle's emphasis on the virtues has been implemented in contemporary critiques of the social and economic system of capitalism,*[11] in approaches to environmental care,[12] and in ethical problems in the medical field.[13] Hence *Nicomachean Ethics* remains—and will remain—one of the most important texts in the history of philosophy.

NOTES

1 Important works are collected in R. Crisp and M. A. Slote, (eds.), *Virtue Ethics* (Oxford: Oxford University Press, 1997).

2 Rosalind Hursthouse, *On Virtue Ethics* (Oxford: Oxford University Press, 2001), 9.

3 Sarah Broadie, "Aristotle and Contemporary Ethics," in *The Blackwell Guide to Aristotle's Nicomachean Ethics*, ed. R. Kraut (Oxford: Wiley-Blackwell, 2006), 344.

4 This claim and the argument supporting it are found in Aristotle, *Nicomachean Ethics*, trans. David Ross, in Aristotle, *Nicomachean Ethics*, trans. Roger Crisp (Cambridge: Cambridge University Press, 2014), I.7.1098a7–20.

5 Compare the virtues discussed in Aristotle, *Nicomachean Ethics*, III.6–V.11.

6 Evidence of such a development of virtue ethics is the publication of Michael Austin, *Virtues in Action: New Essays in Applied Virtue Ethics* (New York: Palgrave Macmillan, 2013).

7 Aristotle, *Nicomachean Ethics*, X.9.1179b21–1180a19.

8 See L. K. Popov, D. Popov and J. Kavelin, *The Family Virtues Guide: Simple Ways to Bring Out the Best in Our Children and Ourselves* (New York: *Plume,* 1997) and Michele Borba, *Building Moral Intelligence: The Seven Essential Virtues that Teach Kids to Do the Right Thing* (Hoboken, NJ: *Jossey-Bass,* 2001).

9 Paula Gottlieb, "Aristotle's Ethics," in *The Oxford Handbook of the History of Ethics*, ed. Roger Crisp (Oxford: Oxford University Press, 2013), 46.

10 Hursthouse, Rosalind, "Virtue Ethics," section 1, in *Stanford Encyclopedia of Philosophy*, ed. Edward N. Zalta (Fall 2013 edn.), accessed February 27, 2016, http://plato.stanford.edu/archives/fall2013/entries/ethics-virtue/.

11 See, for example, Paul Blackledge and Kelvin Knight (eds.), *Virtue and Politics: Alasdair MacIntyre's Revolutionary Aristotelianism* (Notre Dame, IN: University of Notre Dame Press, 2011).

12 See, for example, Ronald Sandler, *Character and Environment: A Virtue-Oriented Approach to Environmental Ethics* (NY: Columbia University Press, 2007).

13 See, for example, Rosalind Hursthouse, "Virtue Theory and Abortion," *Philosophy and Public Affairs* 20, no. 3 (1991): 223–46.

GLOSSARY

GLOSSARY OF TERMS

Academy: an institution for philosophical and mathematical research founded by Plato in Athens probably in the mid-380s B.C.E.

Akrasia: a Greek word meaning "weakness of will" or "lack of mastery"; it is often translated as "incontinence." *Akrasia* is a character trait of people who seem to know the right thing to do but fail to do it.

Ambulatory: a covered area where people could walk around.

Andreia: the Greek word that, in Plato's writings, is often translated as "courage."

Anthropology: the study of human nature. "An anthropology" is a set of beliefs about what human beings are, and it often includes a notion of what allows human beings to flourish.

Aretê: a Greek word that means, literally, "excellence," most often translated in Plato and Aristotle's writings as "virtue."

Biology: the systematic study of all forms of organic life. Aristotle's biology was focused on the observation and classification of many types of marine, plant, and mammalian life.

Capitalism: a social and economic system, dominant in the West today, in which trade and industry are held in private hands and conducted for private profit.

Consequentialism: consequentialist ethics judges the morality of an action on the basis of its consequences.

Contemplation: intellectual reflection upon eternal truths. For Aristotle, contemplation is the best of activities for a human being, and the attribute that makes them unlike animals and like divine beings.

Corpus: the body of written work an author produces over his or her lifetime.

Democracy: a form of political organization in which individual citizens rule through voting for certain laws or certain representatives; the word comes from the Greek meaning "power of the people."

Dikaiosune: an ancient Greek word referring to the virtue of justice.

Doctrine: a philosophical doctrine is a claim that a philosopher is convinced is true; philosophical "doctrines" can be overturned by reason and argumentation.

Endoxa: a term employed by Aristotle to refer to certain opinions commonly held by the majority of the people that have passed the test of time. *Endoxa* are the starting point of moral philosophy, whose task is to make sense of them within a coherent theory.

Enlightenment: a period of rapid and widespread intellectual and cultural development in the Western world. It lasted from approximately 1650 to 1800 and brought tremendous changes in philosophy, politics, economics, and society.

Epicureanism: one of the great ancient philosophical schools founded by Epicurus (341–270 B.C.E.). Its main characteristics are materialism, and pleasure as the highest good.

Ergon: an ancient Greek word meaning "function." This concept is the basis of Aristotle's argument that the function of human beings determines the nature of the ethical life.

Ethics: the subfield of philosophy that seeks to answer the question "How should one live?" It often focuses on concepts such as right and wrong action, the virtues, and moral duty.

Eudaimonia: the end or goal toward which Aristotle argues all human life and action is aimed. It is often translated as "happiness" or "well-being" but lies somewhere between the two; like "happiness," *eudaimonia* is a state that only conscious human beings possess; like "well-being," *eudaimonia* is an objective quality of certain lives.

Hedone: Greek word for "pleasure." The word *hedonism*—seeking everything for the sake of pleasure—comes from this Greek word.

Hellenistic period (322–31 B.C.E.): a historical period in ancient Greece, during which culture and politics thrived. It ended in 31 B.C.E. when ancient Greece was displaced by the Roman Empire.

Incontinence: a common English translation of the Greek word *akrasia*, meaning "weakness of will" or "lack of mastery"—a character trait of people who seem to know the right thing to do but fail to do it.

Kantian ethics: an ethical system that follows the thought of the eighteenth-century philosopher Immanuel Kant. It is aimed at providing universal rules for action, and it proposes that an action is immoral if it cannot be willed to be done universally.

Logic: the subfield of philosophy, begun by Aristotle, which studies the nature and grounds of deductive and inductive reasoning. Aristotle's logic was focused on the strict logical relationship between terms, but logic has become much broader since Aristotle.

Lyceum: the philosophical school founded by Aristotle and in which he wrote several of his major works. It was based in Athens and continued after his death.

Mean: a mathematical term that refers to the middle between two extremes. Here the term is used non-mathematically, to mean a desirable middle ground.

Medieval/Middle Ages: the period in Western European history from about 500 C.E. to 1500 C.E. Beginning with the fall of the Roman Empire, it was a period in which both the Roman Catholic Church and Aristotle greatly influenced the realms of politics, science, and philosophy.

Megalopsuchia: literally "great-souledness"—a crowning virtue within Aristotle's system signifying the character of a person who possesses all of the other virtues, is aware of that fact, and is concerned with great expressions of honor toward himself.

Metaphysics: the subfield of philosophy focused on the nature of reality. Its literal meaning is "after physics" because Aristotle's book on the nature of reality was placed after his book on physics.

Moral philosophy: The subfield of philosophy that focuses on both the theoretical and the practical aspects of morality. It seeks primarily to answer the questions "What is the nature of the good life?" and "How ought we to live?"

Neo-Aristotelians: a group of scholars who have sought to revive Aristotle's ideas in the twentieth century. They believe in virtue ethics, an ethical theory that maintains that virtues play a central or independent role in the behavior of a person and in the moral judgment of an action.

Peloponnesian War (431–404 B.C.E.): a war fought between the city-state of Athens and its allies and the city-state of Sparta and its allies; the Spartans prevailed. The longest conflict in Greek history, it ultimately led to the weakening of the Greek cities and to their fall to foreign domination in the first century B.C.E.

Peripatetics: the followers of Aristotle; the term is a reference to *peripatos*, the Greek word for walking, possibly in reference to the ambulatory—a covered walking place—near the Lyceum.

Persian Wars: wars fought between the Persian Empire and an alliance of Greek city-states from 499 B.C.E. to 448 B.C.E. The more powerful Persians attempted to capture Athens on several occasions, but they failed to do so.

Phainomena: Greek for "appearances," or things that appear to be the case. Aristotle uses the *phainomena* and the opinions of others as the dual starting points of his philosophical investigations.

Philebus: one of Plato's late dialogues exploring the relationship of pleasure and knowledge to the good life. The speakers in the dialogue are Socrates, Protarchus, and Philebus.

Philosophy: the discipline that applies abstract and practical reasoning to the problems of human life. It addresses questions such as "How do we know the truth?", "What is the good life?", and "What is reality really like?"

Phronesis: Greek for "practical wisdom" or "prudence." Aristotle conceives of *phronesis* as an intellectual virtue that helps us to judge the right thing to do in a certain situation.

Polis: Greek for "city," usually referring to the ancient Greek city-states, such as Athens and Sparta.

Pre-Socratic philosophy: refers to the philosophers before Socrates, from the time of Thales of Miletus (around 624–546 B.C.E.). It includes the schools of Miletus, Pythagoras, Elea, and the Atomists, and individuals such as Heraclitus and Anaxagoras, all interested in investigating the principles of the natural world.

Purposive cause: a cause aimed at bringing about some specific end. Aristotle gives these kinds of causes the name "final causes."

Rationalism: a position that emphasizes the dependence of knowledge on theoretical reason.

Reason: the human faculty of abstract reflection. Reason can be theoretical or practical, and it can deal with relations of ideas as well as with matters of fact.

Renaissance: the period of Western European history from roughly the 1500s to the beginning of the 1700s. Meaning "rebirth," the Renaissance was a period in which philosophers, artists, and authors rediscovered and put to use many of the great literary and artistic works of the Classical period of Greece and Rome.

Rhetoric: the art of persuasion by use of words. Today, it is often used negatively ("empty rhetoric"), but historically it meant good arguments and critical thinking.

Roman period (27 B.C.E.–395 C.E.): a historical period of ancient Rome, where it emerged as a great empire that dominated most of Europe.

Scholasticism: a tradition of philosophical inquiry that dominated Western philosophy in the medieval period. Scholasticism (and scholastics, the name for practitioners of Scholasticism) drew heavily on the works of Plato and Aristotle, and sought to integrate philosophy and Roman Catholic theology.

Skepticism: one of the great ancient philosophical schools, whose beginning is usually linked to the philosophy of Pyrrho of Elis (365–275 B.C.E.). Many variations appeared in history, broadly holding that nothing can be known for certain.

Sophia: Greek for "wisdom." Aristotle uses *sophia* to name the intellectual faculty that helps us discover the most noble and honorable truths—something that philosophers devote themselves to.

Sophist: a professional teacher of the ancient Greek world dedicated to the mastery of excellence in several disciplines, from rhetoric to music. Plato, perhaps unfairly, portrayed the Sophists as lovers of money rather than of wisdom for wisdom's sake, and as being devoted to persuasion rather than to the discovery of truth.

Sophrosune: Greek for "moderation," one of the virtues in Plato's ethical works.

Sparta: an ancient Greek city-state located on the Peloponnese (a peninsula forming the southern part of modern-day Greece). Sparta and Athens were among the most powerful Greek city-states in the ancient world.

Stoicism: one of the great ancient philosophical schools, and perhaps the most influential one. Founded in Athens by Zeno of Citium in the early third century B.C.E., it has a strong moral dimension, and holds that virtue is sufficient to achieve happiness.

Teleological: related to design or purpose.

Temperance: the disposition to abstain from pleasure in the appropriate ways and in the appropriate contexts.

Treatise: a written work that deals thoroughly and systematically with a certain subject matter.

Utilitarianism: a moral philosophy developed in the nineteenth century by the English thinker Jeremy Bentham (1748–1832), which asserts that moral goodness lies exclusively in the maximizing of pleasure and the minimizing of pain for the greatest number of people.

Virtue ethics: also called "virtue-based ethics" and "agent-based ethics," this is an ethical theory that maintains the morality of an action should be judged by the character or virtue of the person, rather than by the outcome of the action (the latter being referred to as "consequentialism").

Virtues: Dispositions of character and action that both partially constitute and make possible the good life for human beings. The virtues were important for almost every ancient moral philosopher's system, and the ancients often agreed in emphasizing practical wisdom, courage, temperance, and justice.

Western world: the civilization centered around Europe and North America that has significant cultural sources in the societies of Ancient Greece, Ancient Rome, and the Christian religion.

PEOPLE MENTIONED IN THE TEXT

Alexander of Aphrodisias was an Aristotelian philosopher and head of the Academy in Athens. He devoted his career to supporting Aristotelian philosophy against Platonism, in the form of numerous commentaries of Aristotle's works.

Alexander the Great (356–323 B.C.E.) was the son of Philip II, King of Macedon. On becoming king, Alexander started an unprecedented military campaign, conquering Persia and Egypt, reaching India, and creating one of the largest empires in the ancient world.

Andronicus of Rhodes is likely to have produced the first reliable edition of Aristotle's works. He was probably one of the leaders of the Lyceum in Athens, though there is little concrete evidence as to when.

Elizabeth Anscombe (1919–2001) was a British analytic philosopher. She worked in a variety of fields, from philosophy of mind to logic and ethics, and decisively contributed to the development of virtue ethics.

Thomas Aquinas (1225–1274) was an Italian theologian and philosopher. A member of the Dominican Order, he is arguably the most important medieval philosopher; in his extensive works he combined and blended Aristotelian philosophy and Christian theology.

August Immanuel Bekker (1785–1871) was a German philosopher and editor; he created the Bekker numbering system used for the works of Aristotle.

Chris Bobonich (b. 1960) is an American philosopher who focuses on ancient philosophy, particularly on Plato.

Sarah Broadie (b. 1941) is a professor of moral philosophy at the University of St. Andrews. Her work focuses primarily on classical philosophy, metaphysics, and ethics.

Nicolaus Copernicus (1473–1543) was a Polish astronomer and mathematician, and author of the celebrated *On the Revolutions of the Celestial Spheres.* At a pivotal moment in the intellectual history of Europe, he contributed to the scientific revolution by proposing a model of the universe with the sun at its center.

René Descartes (1596–1650) was a French philosopher and foundational thinker for modern philosophy. Descartes put forward a philosophical method of systematic doubt, and his most famous works were *Discourse Concerning Method* (1637) and *Meditations on First Philosophy* (1641).

Empedocles (circa 490–430 B.C.E.) was a Greek philosopher who developed the famous theory of the four elements (air, fire, water, earth) by which he sought to explain natural phenomena.

Epicurus (341–270 B.C.E.), founder of Epicureanism, was a Greek philosopher. He founded a philosophical school called "the Garden" in Athens, where, until his death, he thought and wrote down his philosophy in the form of letters.

Eudoxus of Cnidus (408–355 B.C.E.) was a Greek astronomer and mathematician. He was Plato's student and one of the greatest classical mathematicians.

Philippa Foot (1920–2010) was a British philosopher. She is best known for her work in virtue ethics.

Dorothea Frede (b. 1941) is a scholar in Classical philosophy. She is the Mills Adjunct Professor of Philosophy at the University of California at Berkeley and professor emeritus at the University of Hamburg; her primary works are on Plato, Aristotle, and Martin Heidegger.

Galileo Galilei (1564–1642) was an Italian astronomer and mathematician. One of the key figures of the scientific revolution, he was the first to observe Jupiter's satellites. He also developed modern mechanics and defended the correct belief that the earth revolves round the sun, for which he was persecuted by the Roman Catholic Church.

Paula Gottlieb is a professor of philosophy at the University of Wisconsin. Her research focuses on Aristotle's ethics and metaphysics.

Heraclitus of Ephesus (circa 535–475 B.C.E.) was a Greek philosopher. He wrote philosophy in the form of short, puzzling sentences, in which he insisted on perennial (continual) change in the natural world.

Thomas Hobbes (1588–1679) was an important philosopher in England, best known for his work in political philosophy, most notably *Leviathan* (1651).

David Hume (1711–76) was a Scottish-born philosopher and historian who played a prominent role in deemphasizing Aristotle.

Rosalind Hursthouse (b. 1943) is a philosopher from New Zealand. She has followed the path of her mentors, Anscombe and Foot, in developing virtue ethics.

Terence Irwin (b. 1947) is a professor of ancient philosophy at Oxford University. His work focuses primarily on how ethics developed in the ancient world.

Immanuel Kant (1724–1804) was a German Enlightenment philosopher. He wrote the celebrated *Critique of Pure Reason* and *Critique of Practical Reason*, originated the Kantian school, and decisively influenced German Idealism and ethics.

Alasdair MacIntyre (b. 1929) is a Scottish philosopher and senior research fellow at London Metropolitan University. His 1981 text *After Virtue* is considered groundbreaking.

J. L. Mackie (1917–81) was an Australian philosopher who specialized in moral and political philosophy. His most important works include *The Miracle of Theism* (1982) and *Ethics: Inventing Right and Wrong* (1977).

Albertus Magnus (1200–1280) is the Latin name for "Albert the Great"—one of the most important Roman Catholic philosophers and theologians in the Middle Ages. He helped integrate Aristotle's teaching into Catholic Christianity, and his most important works include two commentaries on Aristotle's *Nicomachean Ethics*.

Martha Nussbaum (b. 1947) is an American philosopher. She has worked in ancient philosophy, political philosophy, feminism, and animal rights; she is highly influential both within and outside of the academic world.

Parmenides of Elea (b. circa 540 B.C.E.) was a Greek philosopher. He is one of the most influential pre-Socratic philosophers, and he argued for the metaphysical unity of all reality, whose distinctions and differences are only appearances.

Plato (427–347 B.C.E.) was a Greek philosopher. Founder of the Academy in Athens, and one of the greatest philosophers of the Western tradition, he was a disciple of Socrates and teacher of Aristotle. He wrote the great *Dialogues* (including *Republic* and *Symposium*) that set the agenda for Western philosophy.

Ronald Polansky (b. 1949) is a professor of philosophy at Duquesne University and the editor of the journal *Ancient Philosophy*.

Anthony Preus is a professor of philosophy at Binghamton University, where he teaches courses on ancient philosophy and the works of Aristotle, Plato, and Socrates.

Socrates (469–399 B.C.E.) was an Athenian philosopher and the teacher of Plato. He was sentenced to death in 399 B.C.E. on charges of introducing new gods and corrupting the youth. While he did not leave any written texts, Plato's account of his philosophical method of searching for the proper definition of things is acknowledged as a pivotal moment in Western philosophy.

Speusippus (circa. 408–339 B.C.E.) was a Greek philosopher. He was Plato's nephew and Plato's first successor as head of the Academy.

Francisco Suarez (1548–1617) was a very influential Spanish theologian and philosopher, whose most famous works include *Metaphysical Disputations* (1597) and *On the Laws* (1612).

Theophrastus (circa 371–circa 287 B.C.E.) was a Greek philosopher, disciple of Aristotle, and successor to Aristotle at his philosophical school, the Lyceum.

Bernard Williams (1929–2003) was a highly influential British moral philosopher in the second half of the twentieth century. His most important works include *Ethics and the Limits of Philosophy* (1985) and *Utilitarianism: For and Against* (1973).

WORKS CITED

WORKS CITED

Anagnostopoulos, Georgios. "Aristotle's Works and the Development of His Thought." In *A Companion to Aristotle*, edited by Georgios Anagnostopoulos. Oxford: Wiley-Blackwell, 2009.

Anscombe, G. E. M. "Modern Moral Philosophy." *Philosophy* 33, no. 124 (1958): 1–19.

Aristotle. *The Complete Works of Aristotle*. Edited by Jonathan Barnes. Princeton, NJ: Princeton University Press, 1991.

Eudemian Ethics. Edited by Brad Inwood and Raphael Woolf. Cambridge: Cambridge University Press, 2013.

Metaphysics. New York: Peripatetic Press, 1979.

Metaphysics. Translated by S. M. Cohen. In *Readings in Ancient Greek Philosophy*, edited by S. Cohen, P. Curd and C. D. C. Reeve. Indianapolis: Hackett, 2005.

Nicomachean Ethics, rev. ed. Translated by Roger Crisp. Cambridge: Cambridge University Press, 2014.

Physics. Lincoln: University of Nebraska, 1961.

Politics. Translated by T. Irwin. In *Readings in Ancient Greek Philosophy*, edited by S. Cohen, P. Curd and C. D. C. Reeve. Indianapolis: Hackett, 2005.

Austin, Michael. *Virtues in Action: New Essays in Applied Virtue Ethics*. New York: Palgrave Macmillan, 2013.

Barnes, Jonathan. *Aristotle Complete Works*. Princeton, NJ: Princeton University Press, 1991.

The Cambridge Companion to Aristotle. Cambridge: Cambridge University Press, 1995.

Blackledge, Paul, and Kelvin Knight (eds.). *Virtue and Politics: Alasdair MacIntyre's Revolutionary Aristotelianism*. Notre Dame, IN: University of Notre Dame Press, 2011.

Bobonich, Chris. "Aristotle's Ethical Treatises." In *The Blackwell Guide to Aristotle's Nicomachean Ethics*, edited by Richard Kraut, 12–36. Oxford: Wiley-Blackwell, 2006.

Borba, Michele. *Building Moral Intelligence: The Seven Essential Virtues that Teach Kids to Do the Right Thing*. Hoboken, NJ: Jossey-Bass, 2001.

Broadie, Sarah. "Aristotle and Contemporary Ethics." In *The Blackwell Guide to Aristotle's Nicomachean Ethics,* edited by Richard Kraut, 342–61. Oxford: Wiley-Blackwell, 2006.

"Philosophical Introduction." In Aristotle, *Nicomachean Ethics,* translated by Sarah Broadie and Christopher Rowe, 9–80. Oxford: Oxford University Press, 2002.

Celano, Anthony. "The Relation of Prudence and *Synderesis* to Happiness in the Medieval Commentaries on Aristotle's Ethics." In *The Reception of Aristotle's Ethics*, edited by Jon Miller, 125–54. Cambridge: Cambridge University Press, 2012.

Cooper, J. M. "Contemplation and Happiness: A Reconsideration." In *Reason and Emotion: Essays on Ancient Moral Psychology and Ethical Theory*. Princeton, NJ: Princeton University Press, 1999.

"The *Magna Moralia* and Aristotle's Moral Philosophy." *American Journal of Philology* (1973): 327–49.

Copleston, Frederick. *A History of Philosophy: Greece and Rome*. London: Continuum Press, 2003.

Crisp, Roger. *Aristotle Nicomachean Ethics*. Cambridge: Cambridge University Press, 2014.

Crisp, Roger, and M. A. Slote (eds.). *Virtue Ethics.* Oxford: Oxford University Press, 1997.

Diogenes Laertius. *Lives of Eminent Philosophers*. Edited by R. D. Hicks. Cambridge, MA: Harvard University Press, 1966.

Finnis, John. "Aquinas's Moral, Political, and Legal Philosophy." In *Stanford Encyclopedia of Philosophy* (Summer 2014 edn.), edited by Edward N. Zalta. Accessed 15 January, 2016. http://plato.stanford.edu/archives/sum2014/entries/aquinas-moral-political/.

Frede, Dorothea. "Pleasure and Pain in Aristotle's Ethics." In *The Blackwell Guide to Aristotle's Nicomachean Ethics*, edited by R. Kraut, 255–75. Oxford: Blackwell Publishing, 2006.

Gauthier, R. A. "Trois commentaries 'averroistes' sur l'Ethique a Nicomaque." *Archives d'histoire doctrinale et litteraire du moyen age* 16, no. 1 (1947–8): 187–336.

Gottlieb, Paula. "Aristotle's Ethics." In *The Oxford Handbook of the History of Ethics*, edited by R. Crisp. Oxford: Oxford University Press, 2013.

Herdt, Jennifer A. "Aquinas's Aristotelian Defense of Martyr Courage." In *Aquinas and the* Nicomachean Ethics, edited by Tobias Hoffman, Jorn Muller and Matthias Perkams. Cambridge: Cambridge University Press, 2013.

95

Hoffmann, Tobias, Jörn Müller and Matthias Perkams (eds.). *Aquinas and the* Nicomachean Ethics. Cambridge: Cambridge University Press, 2013.

Holowchack, M. Andrew. *Happiness and Greek Ethical Thought*. London: Continuum Press, 2005.

Hursthouse, Rosalind. *On Virtue Ethics*. Oxford: Oxford University Press, 2001.

"Virtue Ethics." In *Stanford Encyclopedia of Philosophy* (Fall 2013 edn.), edited by Edward N. Zalta,. Accessed February 27, 2016. http://plato.stanford.edu/archives/fall2013/entries/ethics-virtue/.

"Virtue Theory and Abortion." *Philosophy and Public Affairs* 20, no. 3 (1991): 223–46.

Irwin, Terence. *The Development of Ethics*, vol. 1. Oxford: Oxford University Press, 2007.

Kenny, Anthony. *The Aristotelian Ethics: A Study of the Relationship Between the* Eudemian *and* Nicomachean Ethics *of Aristotle*. Oxford: Clarendon Press, 1978.

Korsgaard, Christine. *Sources of Normativity*. Cambridge: Cambridge University Press, 2012.

Kraut, R. (ed.) *The Blackwell Guide to Aristotle's* Nicomachean Ethics. Oxford: Blackwell, 2006.

"Two Conceptions of Happiness." *The Philosophical Review* 88 (1979): 167–97.

Long, A. A. "Aristotle's Legacy to Stoic Ethics." *Bulletin of the Institute of Classical Study* 15, no. 1 (1968): 72–85.

MacIntyre, Alasdair. *After Virtue*, 3rd edn. Notre Dame: University of Notre Dame Press, 2007.

Whose Justice? Which Rationality? London: Duckworth, 1988.

Mackie, J. L. *Ethics: Inventing Right and Wrong*. London: Penguin, 1977.

McAleer, Sean. "An Aristotelian Account of Virtue Ethics." *Pacific Philosophical Quarterly* 88 (2007): 208–25.

McInerny, Ralph, and John O'Callaghan. "Saint Thomas Aquinas." In *Stanford Encyclopedia of Philosophy* (May 23, 2014). Edited by Edward N. Zalta. Accessed December 10, 2015. http://plato.stanford.edu/entries/aquinas/#ThoAri.

Mourelatos, Alexander (ed.) *The Pre-Socratics: A Collection of Critical Essays*. Princeton, NJ: Princeton University Press, 1993.

Nielsen, Karen M. "The *Nicomachean Ethics* in Hellenistic Philosophy—A Hidden Treasure?" In *The Reception of Aristotle's Ethics,* edited by Jon Miller, 5–30. Cambridge: Cambridge University Press, 2012.

Nussbaum, M. C. "Non-Relative Virtues: An Aristotelian Approach." In *The Quality of Life*, edited by M. C. Nussbaum and A. Sen, 242–69. Oxford: Clarendon Press, 1993.

"Non-Relative Virtues: An Aristotelian Approach." *Midwest Studies in Philosophy* 13, no. 1 (1998): 34.

"Virtue Ethics: A Misleading Category?" *Journal of Ethics* 3, no. 3 (1999): 163–201.

Plato. *The Republic*. Translated by G. M. A. Grube. In *Readings in Ancient Greek Philosophy*, edited by S. Cohen, P. Curd and C. D. C. Reeve. Indianapolis: Hackett, 2005.

Polansky, Ronald (ed.) *The Cambridge Companion to Aristotle's* Nicomachean Ethics. Cambridge: Cambridge University Press, 2014.

"Introduction: Ethics as Practical Science." In *The Cambridge Companion to Aristotle's Nicomachean Ethics*, edited by R. Polansky. Cambridge: Cambridge University Press, 2014.

Popov, L.K., D. Popov and J. Kavelin. *The Family Virtues Guide: Simple Ways to Bring out the Best in Our Children and Ourselves*. New York: Plume, 1997.

Preus, Anthony. *Historical Dictionary of Ancient Greek Philosophy*. Lanham, MD: Scarecrow Press, 2007.

Ross, David. *The Nicomachean Ethics of Aristotle*. Claremont, CA: Pomona Press, 2006.

Rowe, C. "A Reply to John Cooper on the Magna Moralia." *American Journal of Philology* (1975): 160–72.

Rutherford, Donald. "The End of Ends? Aristotelian Themes in Early Modern Ethics." In *The Reception of Aristotle's Ethics*, edited by Jon Miller, 194–221. Cambridge: Cambridge University Press, 2013.

Sandler, Ronald. *Character and Environment: A Virtue-Oriented Approach to Environmental Ethics*. New York: Columbia University Press, 2007.

Shields, Christopher. "Aristotle." In *Stanford Encyclopedia of Philosophy* (Fall 2015 edn.). Edited by Edward N. Zalta. Accessed January 15, 2015, http:// plato.stanford.edu/archives/fall2015/entries/aristotle/.

Williams, Bernard. *Ethics and the Limits of Philosophy*. London: Routledge, 200

THE MACAT LIBRARY
BY DISCIPLINE

AFRICANA STUDIES

Chinua Achebe's *An Image of Africa: Racism in Conrad's Heart of Darkness*
W. E. B. Du Bois's *The Souls of Black Folk*
Zora Neale Huston's *Characteristics of Negro Expression*
Martin Luther King Jr's *Why We Can't Wait*
Toni Morrison's *Playing in the Dark: Whiteness in the American Literary Imagination*

ANTHROPOLOGY

Arjun Appadurai's *Modernity at Large: Cultural Dimensions of Globalisation*
Philippe Ariès's *Centuries of Childhood*
Franz Boas's *Race, Language and Culture*
Kim Chan & Renée Mauborgne's *Blue Ocean Strategy*
Jared Diamond's *Guns, Germs & Steel: the Fate of Human Societies*
Jared Diamond's *Collapse: How Societies Choose to Fail or Survive*
E. E. Evans-Pritchard's *Witchcraft, Oracles and Magic Among the Azande*
James Ferguson's *The Anti-Politics Machine*
Clifford Geertz's *The Interpretation of Cultures*
David Graeber's *Debt: the First 5000 Years*
Karen Ho's *Liquidated: An Ethnography of Wall Street*
Geert Hofstede's *Culture's Consequences: Comparing Values, Behaviors, Institutes and Organizations across Nations*
Claude Lévi-Strauss's *Structural Anthropology*
Jay Macleod's *Ain't No Makin' It: Aspirations and Attainment in a Low-Income Neighborhood*
Saba Mahmood's *The Politics of Piety: The Islamic Revival and the Feminist Subjec*t
Marcel Mauss's *The Gift*

BUSINESS

Jean Lave & Etienne Wenger's *Situated Learning*
Theodore Levitt's *Marketing Myopia*
Burton G. Malkiel's *A Random Walk Down Wall Street*
Douglas McGregor's *The Human Side of Enterprise*
Michael Porter's *Competitive Strategy: Creating and Sustaining Superior Performance*
John Kotter's *Leading Change*
C. K. Prahalad & Gary Hamel's *The Core Competence of the Corporation*

CRIMINOLOGY

Michelle Alexander's *The New Jim Crow: Mass Incarceration in the Age of Colorblindness*
Michael R. Gottfredson & Travis Hirschi's *A General Theory of Crime*
Richard Herrnstein & Charles A. Murray's *The Bell Curve: Intelligence and Class Structure in American Life*
Elizabeth Loftus's *Eyewitness Testimony*
Jay Macleod's *Ain't No Makin' It: Aspirations and Attainment in a Low-Income Neighborhood*
Philip Zimbardo's *The Lucifer Effect*

ECONOMICS

Janet Abu-Lughod's *Before European Hegemony*
Ha-Joon Chang's *Kicking Away the Ladder*
David Brion Davis's *The Problem of Slavery in the Age of Revolution*
Milton Friedman's *The Role of Monetary Policy*
Milton Friedman's *Capitalism and Freedom*
David Graeber's *Debt: the First 5000 Years*
Friedrich Hayek's *The Road to Serfdom*
Karen Ho's *Liquidated: An Ethnography of Wall Street*

John Maynard Keynes's *The General Theory of Employment, Interest and Money*
Charles P. Kindleberger's *Manias, Panics and Crashes*
Robert Lucas's *Why Doesn't Capital Flow from Rich to Poor Countries?*
Burton G. Malkiel's *A Random Walk Down Wall Street*
Thomas Robert Malthus's *An Essay on the Principle of Population*
Karl Marx's *Capital*
Thomas Piketty's *Capital in the Twenty-First Century*
Amartya Sen's *Development as Freedom*
Adam Smith's *The Wealth of Nations*
Nassim Nicholas Taleb's *The Black Swan: The Impact of the Highly Improbable*
Amos Tversky's & Daniel Kahneman's *Judgment under Uncertainty: Heuristics and Biases*
Mahbub Ul Haq's *Reflections on Human Development*
Max Weber's *The Protestant Ethic and the Spirit of Capitalism*

FEMINISM AND GENDER STUDIES

Judith Butler's *Gender Trouble*
Simone De Beauvoir's *The Second Sex*
Michel Foucault's *History of Sexuality*
Betty Friedan's *The Feminine Mystique*
Saba Mahmood's *The Politics of Piety: The Islamic Revival and the Feminist Subject*
Joan Wallach Scott's *Gender and the Politics of History*
Mary Wollstonecraft's *A Vindication of the Rights of Women*
Virginia Woolf's *A Room of One's Own*

GEOGRAPHY

The Brundtland Report's *Our Common Future*
Rachel Carson's *Silent Spring*
Charles Darwin's *On the Origin of Species*
James Ferguson's *The Anti-Politics Machine*
Jane Jacobs's *The Death and Life of Great American Cities*
James Lovelock's *Gaia: A New Look at Life on Earth*
Amartya Sen's *Development as Freedom*
Mathis Wackernagel & William Rees's *Our Ecological Footprint*

HISTORY

Janet Abu-Lughod's *Before European Hegemony*
Benedict Anderson's *Imagined Communities*
Bernard Bailyn's *The Ideological Origins of the American Revolution*
Hanna Batatu's *The Old Social Classes And The Revolutionary Movements Of Iraq*
Christopher Browning's *Ordinary Men: Reserve Police Batallion 101 and the Final Solution in Poland*
Edmund Burke's *Reflections on the Revolution in France*
William Cronon's *Nature's Metropolis: Chicago And The Great West*
Alfred W. Crosby's *The Columbian Exchange*
Hamid Dabashi's *Iran: A People Interrupted*
David Brion Davis's *The Problem of Slavery in the Age of Revolution*
Nathalie Zemon Davis's *The Return of Martin Guerre*
Jared Diamond's *Guns, Germs & Steel: the Fate of Human Societies*
Frank Dikotter's *Mao's Great Famine*
John W Dower's *War Without Mercy: Race And Power In The Pacific War*
W. E. B. Du Bois's *The Souls of Black Folk*
Richard J. Evans's *In Defence of History*
Lucien Febvre's *The Problem of Unbelief in the 16th Century*
Sheila Fitzpatrick's *Everyday Stalinism*

Eric Foner's *Reconstruction: America's Unfinished Revolution, 1863-1877*
Michel Foucault's *Discipline and Punish*
Michel Foucault's *History of Sexuality*
Francis Fukuyama's *The End of History and the Last Man*
John Lewis Gaddis's *We Now Know: Rethinking Cold War History*
Ernest Gellner's *Nations and Nationalism*
Eugene Genovese's *Roll, Jordan, Roll: The World the Slaves Made*
Carlo Ginzburg's *The Night Battles*
Daniel Goldhagen's *Hitler's Willing Executioners*
Jack Goldstone's *Revolution and Rebellion in the Early Modern World*
Antonio Gramsci's *The Prison Notebooks*
Alexander Hamilton, John Jay & James Madison's *The Federalist Papers*
Christopher Hill's *The World Turned Upside Down*
Carole Hillenbrand's *The Crusades: Islamic Perspectives*
Thomas Hobbes's *Leviathan*
Eric Hobsbawm's *The Age Of Revolution*
John A. Hobson's *Imperialism: A Study*
Albert Hourani's *History of the Arab Peoples*
Samuel P. Huntington's *The Clash of Civilizations and the Remaking of World Order*
C. L. R. James's *The Black Jacobins*
Tony Judt's *Postwar: A History of Europe Since 1945*
Ernst Kantorowicz's *The King's Two Bodies: A Study in Medieval Political Theology*
Paul Kennedy's *The Rise and Fall of the Great Powers*
Ian Kershaw's *The "Hitler Myth": Image and Reality in the Third Reich*
John Maynard Keynes's *The General Theory of Employment, Interest and Money*
Charles P. Kindleberger's *Manias, Panics and Crashes*
Martin Luther King Jr's *Why We Can't Wait*
Henry Kissinger's *World Order: Reflections on the Character of Nations and the Course of History*
Thomas Kuhn's *The Structure of Scientific Revolutions*
Georges Lefebvre's *The Coming of the French Revolution*
John Locke's *Two Treatises of Government*
Niccolò Machiavelli's *The Prince*
Thomas Robert Malthus's *An Essay on the Principle of Population*
Mahmood Mamdani's *Citizen and Subject: Contemporary Africa And The Legacy Of Late Colonialism*
Karl Marx's *Capital*
Stanley Milgram's *Obedience to Authority*
John Stuart Mill's *On Liberty*
Thomas Paine's *Common Sense*
Thomas Paine's *Rights of Man*
Geoffrey Parker's *Global Crisis: War, Climate Change and Catastrophe in the Seventeenth Century*
Jonathan Riley-Smith's *The First Crusade and the Idea of Crusading*
Jean-Jacques Rousseau's *The Social Contract*
Joan Wallach Scott's *Gender and the Politics of History*
Theda Skocpol's *States and Social Revolutions*
Adam Smith's *The Wealth of Nations*
Timothy Snyder's *Bloodlands: Europe Between Hitler and Stalin*
Sun Tzu's *The Art of War*
Keith Thomas's *Religion and the Decline of Magic*
Thucydides's *The History of the Peloponnesian War*
Frederick Jackson Turner's *The Significance of the Frontier in American History*
Odd Arne Westad's *The Global Cold War: Third World Interventions And The Making Of Our Times*

LITERATURE

Chinua Achebe's *An Image of Africa: Racism in Conrad's Heart of Darkness*
Roland Barthes's *Mythologies*
Homi K. Bhabha's *The Location of Culture*
Judith Butler's *Gender Trouble*
Simone De Beauvoir's *The Second Sex*
Ferdinand De Saussure's *Course in General Linguistics*
T. S. Eliot's *The Sacred Wood: Essays on Poetry and Criticism*
Zora Neale Huston's *Characteristics of Negro Expression*
Toni Morrison's *Playing in the Dark: Whiteness in the American Literary Imagination*
Edward Said's *Orientalism*
Gayatri Chakravorty Spivak's *Can the Subaltern Speak?*
Mary Wollstonecraft's *A Vindication of the Rights of Women*
Virginia Woolf's *A Room of One's Own*

PHILOSOPHY

Elizabeth Anscombe's *Modern Moral Philosophy*
Hannah Arendt's *The Human Condition*
Aristotle's *Metaphysics*
Aristotle's *Nicomachean Ethics*
Edmund Gettier's *Is Justified True Belief Knowledge?*
Georg Wilhelm Friedrich Hegel's *Phenomenology of Spirit*
David Hume's *Dialogues Concerning Natural Religion*
David Hume's *The Enquiry for Human Understanding*
Immanuel Kant's *Religion within the Boundaries of Mere Reason*
Immanuel Kant's *Critique of Pure Reason*
Søren Kierkegaard's *The Sickness Unto Death*
Søren Kierkegaard's *Fear and Trembling*
C. S. Lewis's *The Abolition of Man*
Alasdair MacIntyre's *After Virtue*
Marcus Aurelius's *Meditations*
Friedrich Nietzsche's *On the Genealogy of Morality*
Friedrich Nietzsche's *Beyond Good and Evil*
Plato's *Republic*
Plato's *Symposium*
Jean-Jacques Rousseau's *The Social Contract*
Gilbert Ryle's *The Concept of Mind*
Baruch Spinoza's *Ethics*
Sun Tzu's *The Art of War*
Ludwig Wittgenstein's *Philosophical Investigations*

POLITICS

Benedict Anderson's *Imagined Communities*
Aristotle's *Politics*
Bernard Bailyn's *The Ideological Origins of the American Revolution*
Edmund Burke's *Reflections on the Revolution in France*
John C. Calhoun's *A Disquisition on Government*
Ha-Joon Chang's *Kicking Away the Ladder*
Hamid Dabashi's *Iran: A People Interrupted*
Hamid Dabashi's *Theology of Discontent: The Ideological Foundation of the Islamic Revolution in Iran*
Robert Dahl's *Democracy and its Critics*
Robert Dahl's *Who Governs?*
David Brion Davis's *The Problem of Slavery in the Age of Revolution*

Alexis De Tocqueville's *Democracy in America*
James Ferguson's *The Anti-Politics Machine*
Frank Dikotter's *Mao's Great Famine*
Sheila Fitzpatrick's *Everyday Stalinism*
Eric Foner's *Reconstruction: America's Unfinished Revolution, 1863-1877*
Milton Friedman's *Capitalism and Freedom*
Francis Fukuyama's *The End of History and the Last Man*
John Lewis Gaddis's *We Now Know: Rethinking Cold War History*
Ernest Gellner's *Nations and Nationalism*
David Graeber's *Debt: the First 5000 Years*
Antonio Gramsci's *The Prison Notebooks*
Alexander Hamilton, John Jay & James Madison's *The Federalist Papers*
Friedrich Hayek's *The Road to Serfdom*
Christopher Hill's *The World Turned Upside Down*
Thomas Hobbes's *Leviathan*
John A. Hobson's *Imperialism: A Study*
Samuel P. Huntington's *The Clash of Civilizations and the Remaking of World Order*
Tony Judt's *Postwar: A History of Europe Since 1945*
David C. Kang's *China Rising: Peace, Power and Order in East Asia*
Paul Kennedy's *The Rise and Fall of Great Powers*
Robert Keohane's *After Hegemony*
Martin Luther King Jr.'s *Why We Can't Wait*
Henry Kissinger's *World Order: Reflections on the Character of Nations and the Course of History*
John Locke's *Two Treatises of Government*
Niccolò Machiavelli's *The Prince*
Thomas Robert Malthus's *An Essay on the Principle of Population*
Mahmood Mamdani's *Citizen and Subject: Contemporary Africa And The Legacy Of Late Colonialism*
Karl Marx's *Capital*
John Stuart Mill's *On Liberty*
John Stuart Mill's *Utilitarianism*
Hans Morgenthau's *Politics Among Nations*
Thomas Paine's *Common Sense*
Thomas Paine's *Rights of Man*
Thomas Piketty's *Capital in the Twenty-First Century*
Robert D. Putman's *Bowling Alone*
John Rawls's *Theory of Justice*
Jean-Jacques Rousseau's *The Social Contract*
Theda Skocpol's *States and Social Revolutions*
Adam Smith's *The Wealth of Nations*
Sun Tzu's *The Art of War* .
Henry David Thoreau's *Civil Disobedience*
Thucydides's *The History of the Peloponnesian War*
Kenneth Waltz's *Theory of International Politics*
Max Weber's *Politics as a Vocation*
Odd Arne Westad's *The Global Cold War: Third World Interventions And The Making Of Our Times*

POSTCOLONIAL STUDIES

Roland Barthes's *Mythologies*
Frantz Fanon's *Black Skin, White Masks*
Homi K. Bhabha's *The Location of Culture*
Gustavo Gutiérrez's *A Theology of Liberation*
Edward Said's *Orientalism*
Gayatri Chakravorty Spivak's *Can the Subaltern Speak?*

PSYCHOLOGY

Gordon Allport's *The Nature of Prejudice*
Alan Baddeley & Graham Hitch's *Aggression: A Social Learning Analysis*
Albert Bandura's *Aggression: A Social Learning Analysis*
Leon Festinger's *A Theory of Cognitive Dissonance*
Sigmund Freud's *The Interpretation of Dreams*
Betty Friedan's *The Feminine Mystique*
Michael R. Gottfredson & Travis Hirschi's *A General Theory of Crime*
Eric Hoffer's *The True Believer: Thoughts on the Nature of Mass Movements*
William James's *Principles of Psychology*
Elizabeth Loftus's *Eyewitness Testimony*
A. H. Maslow's *A Theory of Human Motivation*
Stanley Milgram's *Obedience to Authority*
Steven Pinker's *The Better Angels of Our Nature*
Oliver Sacks's *The Man Who Mistook His Wife For a Hat*
Richard Thaler & Cass Sunstein's *Nudge: Improving Decisions About Health, Wealth and Happiness*
Amos Tversky's *Judgment under Uncertainty: Heuristics and Biases*
Philip Zimbardo's *The Lucifer Effect*

SCIENCE

Rachel Carson's *Silent Spring*
William Cronon's *Nature's Metropolis: Chicago And The Great West*
Alfred W. Crosby's *The Columbian Exchange*
Charles Darwin's *On the Origin of Species*
Richard Dawkin's *The Selfish Gene*
Thomas Kuhn's *The Structure of Scientific Revolutions*
Geoffrey Parker's *Global Crisis: War, Climate Change and Catastrophe in the Seventeenth Century*
Mathis Wackernagel & William Rees's *Our Ecological Footprint*

SOCIOLOGY

Michelle Alexander's *The New Jim Crow: Mass Incarceration in the Age of Colorblindness*
Gordon Allport's *The Nature of Prejudice*
Albert Bandura's *Aggression: A Social Learning Analysis*
Hanna Batatu's *The Old Social Classes And The Revolutionary Movements Of Iraq*
Ha-Joon Chang's *Kicking Away the Ladder*
W. E. B. Du Bois's *The Souls of Black Folk*
Émile Durkheim's *On Suicide*
Frantz Fanon's *Black Skin, White Masks*
Frantz Fanon's *The Wretched of the Earth*
Eric Foner's *Reconstruction: America's Unfinished Revolution, 1863-1877*
Eugene Genovese's *Roll, Jordan, Roll: The World the Slaves Made*
Jack Goldstone's *Revolution and Rebellion in the Early Modern World*
Antonio Gramsci's *The Prison Notebooks*
Richard Herrnstein & Charles A Murray's *The Bell Curve: Intelligence and Class Structure in American Life*
Eric Hoffer's *The True Believer: Thoughts on the Nature of Mass Movements*
Jane Jacobs's *The Death and Life of Great American Cities*
Robert Lucas's *Why Doesn't Capital Flow from Rich to Poor Countries?*
Jay Macleod's *Ain't No Makin' It: Aspirations and Attainment in a Low Income Neighborhood*
Elaine May's *Homeward Bound: American Families in the Cold War Era*
Douglas McGregor's *The Human Side of Enterprise*
C. Wright Mills's *The Sociological Imagination*

Thomas Piketty's *Capital in the Twenty-First Century*
Robert D. Putman's *Bowling Alone*
David Riesman's *The Lonely Crowd: A Study of the Changing American Character*
Edward Said's *Orientalism*
Joan Wallach Scott's *Gender and the Politics of History*
Theda Skocpol's *States and Social Revolutions*
Max Weber's *The Protestant Ethic and the Spirit of Capitalism*

THEOLOGY

Augustine's *Confessions*
Benedict's *Rule of St Benedict*
Gustavo Gutiérrez's *A Theology of Liberation*
Carole Hillenbrand's *The Crusades: Islamic Perspectives*
David Hume's *Dialogues Concerning Natural Religion*
Immanuel Kant's *Religion within the Boundaries of Mere Reason*
Ernst Kantorowicz's *The King's Two Bodies: A Study in Medieval Political Theology*
Søren Kierkegaard's *The Sickness Unto Death*
C. S. Lewis's *The Abolition of Man*
Saba Mahmood's *The Politics of Piety: The Islamic Revival and the Feminist Subject*
Baruch Spinoza's *Ethics*
Keith Thomas's *Religion and the Decline of Magic*

COMING SOON

Chris Argyris's *The Individual and the Organisation*
Seyla Benhabib's *The Rights of Others*
Walter Benjamin's *The Work Of Art in the Age of Mechanical Reproduction*
John Berger's *Ways of Seeing*
Pierre Bourdieu's *Outline of a Theory of Practice*
Mary Douglas's *Purity and Danger*
Roland Dworkin's *Taking Rights Seriously*
James G. March's *Exploration and Exploitation in Organisational Learning*
Ikujiro Nonaka's *A Dynamic Theory of Organizational Knowledge Creation*
Griselda Pollock's *Vision and Difference*
Amartya Sen's *Inequality Re-Examined*
Susan Sontag's *On Photography*
Yasser Tabbaa's *The Transformation of Islamic Art*
Ludwig von Mises's *Theory of Money and Credit*